This new raspberries book has 140 delectable recipes, gourmet to common, many made with nonfat cooking ingredients. This is a big consideration these days when we prepare meals, especially dessert.

Barbara Kimball, Manager -Cooksmart, Cherry Creek, Colorado

The herbal & homeopathic characteristics, the preparation for childbirth tips, year-round cultivation procedures, the buying and storing techniques and fat-reducing cooking tips are a real plus.

Jennifer Workman, M.S.R.D., Alfalfas, Denver, Colorado

Multicultural cooking has always been a strong interest. France, the Provence region, has been a major area of inspiration. Features of low fat and nonfat French desserts, adapted and **made healthy**, are revealed in French Pudding, souffle with Framboise Sauce and others. There are Austrian classics such as Molded Bavarian Cream and Red Raspberry Pie. The many Scandinavian recipes from the Pacific Northwest were passed on by an adored aunt Lillian.

Born and fed in Colorado, the author's, Vivian Brock, interest in cooking started as a little girl, spending time with four aunts who cooked with berries and the fresh produce from their own farms. She grew up and became an art teacher with a focus on other cultures. This led her to travel the world collecting recipes and artifacts to share with her students and her 14 grandchildren.

The beginning of the cookbook developed from a small collection of near-forgotten family favorites, Vivian wrote for her mother and a close friend at Christmas in 1987. Since then, she has been collecting materials for a more complete *"raspberry lover"* book and adding illustrations of the many animals that have visited her *"patch"*.

Lucy Hartman, Co-Chair Colorado Gourmet Society

A guide to cultivating &
enjoying raspberries

Raspberry
Story

Includes 140 Recipes
Hot Tips & Sound Advice

Vivian Brock

Copyright © 1997 by Vivian Brock

All rights reserved.

Illustrated by Vivian Brock

Printed in Canada

Printed by Métrolitho

Typesetting by Mountain Media, Conifer, Colorado

First Edition

ISBN   0-9657668-4-5

Library of Congress Catalog Card Number   97-93953

Vivian Brock

1000 E. Stanford Ave.

Englewood CO 80110

Expression of Appreciation

to my Aunt Lillian,
who inspired me and introduced me
to know and love raspberries. Many thanks
to friends and family who contributed
recipes and technical advice for
our Raspberries book.
Write to me.
Enjoy!

CONTENTS

THE RASPBERRY STORY

The Raspberry Treasure

I'll bet you have heard the saying made by a famous beauty, that "It's impossible to be too rich or too thin". Then there are those of us who would say "..... or to have too many raspberries".

The crown jewels of America's native fruits, ruby-red, golden -orange, or almost black, they are the most elegant of the bramble bush tribe, and cousins of two other favorites, the rose and the hearty blackberry.

Wild red raspberries are found for the picking, in the mountains, and in the woods across the United States. The hybridized descendants of the native species, rule without challenge over all the fruits brought into the market place; though they are many times, scarce, having to be flown in from a summer place elsewhere, and also expensive.

Rubus idaeus "The fruit is good to be given to those that have weake and queasie stomackes."
John Gerard 1597.

Raspberry is a member of the rose family. It is a hardy perennial, growing from three to six feet in height. The canes or stems are covered with tiny thorns, and the broad leaves are green on the top and gray-green and have a velvety texture underneath. The flowers are small white and rose like blooming from May through July. Fruits arrive from July to October. The leaves can be collected and dried through out the season but it is believed that they are the most potent when the raspberry is flowering. Perhaps it is best then, to harvest leaves during summer before fruit ripens.

The raspberry's character is dry, astringent, and generally cooling. Its constituents: The leaves have fragarine (uterine tonic), tannins, and polypeptides. The fruit contains vitamins A, B, C, E, sugars, minerals, volatile oil.

Actions from the leaves include childbirth preparation, stimulant, digestive remedy and tonic. The leaves are useful for wounds and for sore throats and mouth ulcers. The leaves have been included in rheumatic remedies as a cleansing diuretic and in France they are regarded as a tonic for the prostate gland.

RASPBERRY THE HERB

The wild raspberry plant's genus name is Rubus, meaning "red". The species are many such as Rubus idaeus and Rubus stigosus, but most herbalists agree that all the red raspberry plants do share common uses and so refer to them as the Rubus species.

Raspberries are used to support and nourish mothers during pregnancy. This shrub, a favorite of mothers, is rich in nutrients and therefore has been used as a folk medicine, by women particularly, for centuries.

The herbal use for pregnancy is global. Europe, Asia, North and South America, have been using the raspberry tea for pregnant women for so many hundreds of years. "A tea made from red raspberry leaves is the best gift God ever gave to Woman." is the quote by Henry Box, and 19th century herbalist. And when we look at the properties of the leaves we do agree, as they include:

Alterative: Helps alter the path of disease by restoring healthy functions of the body.

Antiabortive: Aids mothers in avoiding miscarriage in that it helps prevent uterine spasms (Lancet, II: 6149:I).

Antiseptic: Wards off infection by inhibiting microorganisms.

Astringent: Helps contract and tighten tissue and blood vessels.

Homeostatic: Can help stop excessive bleeding.

Parturient: Facilitates the birth process.

Tonic: In the case of promoting healthy tone the leaves help the adrenals, kidneys, liver, uterus and mucous membranes.

These wonder leaves are rich in calcium and magnesium. The magnesium content being especially important in strengthening the uterine muscle and contain vitamins E, B3, and B1. The minerals selenium sulfur, potassium and phosphorus are found too in small amounts. Other beneficial constituents also include volatile oils, malic acid, organic acids, 90 percent of which is citric acid, and tannic acid.

TRADITIONAL USES

Traditionally the fruit is taken for indigestion and rheumatism. The berries, rich in vitamins and minerals and are highly nutritious. The fruit acts as a diuretic, laxative, diaphoretic, and cleansing agent. The juice has been used in folk medicine as a cooling remedy for fevers, childhood illnesses and cystitus.

RASPBERRY TEA
1 cup of water
1 heaping teaspoon dried raspberry leaf

To make a cup of the raspberry tea, you bring one cup of water to a boil. Remove from the heat and add one heaping teaspoon of the herb, stir, cover, and let stand for approximately 10 minutes. Do not boil the herb. Strain the tea and it is ready. One can make the tea ahead and have it ready for several days: Funnel extra tea in a glass container with a cover and store in the refrigerator and then reheat, or drink it cool.

THE RASPBERRY PLANT AS A HOUSEHOLD REMEDY

Raspberry vinegars are used for coughs as well as sore throats. The leaves, used in infusions, can help diarrhea or if used in poultices, soothe hemorrhoids. The leaves contain raw materials that help the body produce its own estrogen. Subsequently raspberry leaves, when used as tea, could be considered as an additional estrogen replacement. Raspberry syrup is used to prevent a buildup of tartar. Gerard considered the fruit "of a temperate heat" so it was easier on the stomach than strawberries, which could cause excess phlegm and chilling.

LEAVES

INFUSION

Tonifies the uterus to ease labor. Use for diarrhea, gargle for mouth ulcers and sore throat, thematic remedies, cleansing diuretic, tonic for prostrate gland.

Standard quantities: 30 grams dried herb or 75 grams fresh herb to 500 ml water. Standard dose: 1/2 cup three times a day. Equipment: kettle or teapot, nylon sieve or strainer, teacup, covered pitcher for storage.

TINCTURE

Any part of the plant may be used. More astringent than the infusion, the diluted tincture is used on wounds and inflammations or as a mouthwash for ulcer and gum inflammation. This is made by steeping the dried or fresh herb in a 25% mixture of water or vodka. Besides extracting the plant's active ingredients, the vodka acts as a preservative. Tinctures will keep for up to two years.

Standard quantities: 200 grams dried herb or 600 fresh herb to 1 liter water mixture, 1/2 water and 1/2 vodka. Equipment: large screw-top jar, jelly bag or cheesecloth, wine press, large pitcher, funnel and dark glass bottles with screw caps for airtight storage.

WASH

Use the infusion for washing wounds. Apply often to sores and varicose ulcers. Infusions can be used to treat eyes; making a soothing eyewash. Infusions or diluted tinctures can be used on other problems mentioned above. Soak a pad of cotton in the wash and bathe the affected area from the center outward. Alternatively, use a plastic atomizer to spray the herb mixture on varicose ulcers or rashes.

BERRIES

VINEGAR

Steep 500 grams fruit in one liter of wine vinegar for 24 hours then strain through a cheese cloth. This thick red liquid can be added to cough mixtures or used in gargles for sore throats. Its pleasant taste can help disguise the flavor of other herbal expectorants.

THE FOOD VALUE OF RASPBERRIES

The A-Z Healing food book has included raspberries as one of their valued foods. Raspberries have 60-70 calories per cup; a cup of black raspberries has 98 calories. Their carbohydrate content is 6 percent.

Raspberries contain 53% of RDA in vitamin C. Just a couple handfuls as a snack or on top of cereal can give you the bulk of your vitamin C for the day.

If you are wanting to reduce your calorie intake, they are an ideal low-calorie sweet.

"Fiber is beneficial for digestion, absorption and good elimination, which in turn, strengthens the immune system. Increased fiber gives one the feeling of being satiated or *full* and don't we eat less when we feel full? Raspberries put alkaline in the blood. For the arthritic person, this added alkaline is a welcome addition to their daily diet. "

Jennifer Workman, M.S.R.D.

The insoluble fiber that you get from raspberries and blackberries is ideal. It is right up there with that of the whole grains. You say you don't like the seeds between your teeth, then put the berries through a strainer! Strained they retain the food value and loose most of the fiber.

The berries help with blood pressure. Research by University of Mississippi's Dr. Lanagain reports that our blood pressure troubles may be due not simply to too much sodium, but also to the dietary patterns which potassium, sodium's co-worker, is consumed in amounts too small to maintain the healthy balance of potassium with almost no sodium. A healthy dietary dietary pattern is to maintain a healthy balance between these two minerals. Berries do provide a healthy amount of potassium with almost no sodium, they can help restore a better balance between these two nutrients and help our blood pressure. Now measure all their merits, a fair amount of iron, low fat, fiber, potassium, no sodium. They are the perfect food for the heart.

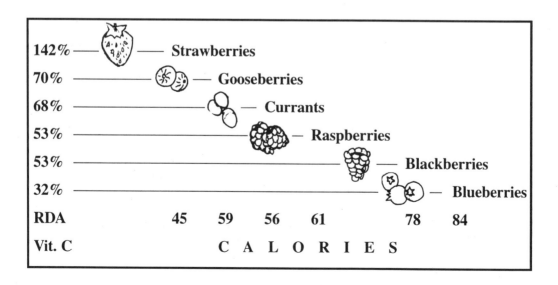

142% — Strawberries						
70% — Gooseberries						
68% — Currants						
53% — Raspberries						
53% — Blackberries						
32% — Blueberries						
RDA	45	59	56	61	78	84
Vit. C	C A L O R I E S					

FEMALE HOMEOPATHY

FERTILITY

More benefits in the leaves include:

an increase in fertility for both men and women
helps to prevent both spotting and miscarriage
reduces both false labor and childbirth pain
reduces hypertension
decreases risk of postpartum hemorrhaging
lessens the swelling of the uterus
increases colostrum in mother's milk
induces the body to produce its own estrogen

The leaves help alleviate menstrual cramps, curb menstrual flow and can be used for a douche. Childrens' diarrhea and fevers can be helped by raspberry tea.

PREGNANCY

During pregnancy, the raspberry is so important for many reason, calcium and magnesium are vital for nourishing for fetal skeleton and to help prevent leg cramps in the mother. Iron, easily assimilated from the raspberry helps prevent anemia. It works to relieve morning sickness and especially if combined with a little ginger and peppermint leaf. While the abundance of minerals and vitamins are impressive, there is the alkaloid fragarine which is believed to contribute to the raspberry's tonifying properties on the smooth muscles of the uterus. The tannic acid is also a tonic property of the herb. The tea has no caffeine. The taste is mildly bitter and sour but not unpleasant.

In the book, *Healing Yourself During Pregnancy* (Crossing Press), the author J. Gardner, suggests that if you start drinking raspberry tea in your first trimester, drink just one cup daily. As you begin your second trimester, drink two cups and drink three cups if you wait until the final trimester. The best plan is to start drinking red raspberry tea as early in the pregnancy as possible. However, when nursing is established, excess consumption of raspberry leaf should be avoided because the astringent properties could reduce the amount of breast milk production. There are capsules and tinctures available to those who do not like drinking tea. Do use organic raspberry tea regardless of the form that you decide upon.

In Chinese medicine, the raspberry leaf is thought of as a tonic for yin. Ayurvedic medicine considers the properties of the tea to decrease the water and fire elements while increasing the air in the elements of the body.

Please do check with your physician before embarking on any herbal regime, especially when pregnant.

PATCH OF YOUR OWN

Cultivating Raspberries

The raspberry has been cultivated since the mid-sixteenth century and no doubt had an easier existence in those days. Today, due to problems with plant viruses, the need for hand care of the vines and hand-picking along with the perishability of the fruits (they crush and mold quickly), there are few fresh raspberries available and those that are cost plenty. Even in the peak season, July, a half pint, actually 6 ounces, can cost $3 or more. Get your berries from a farm or farm stand and they will likely be as fresh and cheaper.

Unlucky for us the raspberry is not a good traveler and does not keep for a very long time. Because of this fragility, and therefore costliness at the fruit stand, many people are cultivating them in their own gardens over much of the country. So if you're thinking of growing your own patch, it is quite feasible in most of the cooler regions of the country, particularly in the mild costal and mountain climates of the West and Northwest and generally north of the Potomac River and the Ohio Valley. Raspberries do not do well in the conditions that exist in the hottest and dampest regions of the South, or the desert regions or the in extremely cold dry parts of the Great Plains. They do very well in Colorado.

The Garden-Nursery catalogs offer guidelines on varieties th at are suited to different growing regions. These include, besides the familiar red berry, yellow ones from pale to amber; the intensely flavorful purple raspberry, a cross between red and black; and the black or blackcap, which is especially excellent for jelly and preserves.

Occasionally, pinkish-yellow raspberries, called honeyberries, reach the fresh market; these are, some say, the most succulent of the lot. The English gardeners have the fabled white raspberry which is cherished and rare in Britain. Our shores have not established this white variety.

Specific information for your own region can be secured from your state agricultural experiment station or extension service. In Colorado, for Denver County, call 640-5270, for Arapahoe County call 730-1920, and ask for the Master Gardner Program.

If you live in the mid- to upper regions of the South, the good news is that progress has given us some hybrids such as the Southland Raspberry, an everbearing red fruit.

It is easy enough to expect approximately a quart of berries a year from each foot of a row. The plants will need a sunny spot with well drained soil that is not too alkaline. You simply plant, water, mulch, prune and pick; mother nature will do her miracle.

FALL

Fall is the ideal time for starting the patch. Picking out the spot described above and securing healthy starters from a friend, neighbor or the local nursery. Red raspberries grow in most garden soils provided they are amply supplied with organic matter and adequately drained. Combine weathered manure, sphagnum peat moss or compost with well-spaded soil to create conditions that ensure a steady harvest of large berries.

If summer-bearing raspberries are planted on a good garden soil, apply only a maintenance amount of fertilizer, consisting of four pounds of ammonium sulfate and two pounds of treble superphosphate, 1 pound of zinc sulfate, 1 pound of iron chelate and 10 bushels of organic matter per 1,000 square feet. Work these amendments in before planting. If fall-bearers are grown, increase the amounts of fertilizer by 50%.

Maintain fertility with a spring application of 4 pounds of ammonium sulfate and 2 pounds of treble super phosphate per 1,000 square feet. Scatter among the canes and cultivate into the soil. Raspberries should receive enough water to maintain a moderate moisture level in their root zone.

A planting site that receives only morning or afternoon sun will work as well as all day sun. Do not plant raspberries under shade trees; tree roots compete for water and nutrients that raspberries need. The canes need to be planted 3 feet apart; multiple canes will soon grow from each original.

TRELLISING

Fall-bearing raspberries seldom require trellising; however, summer-bearing varieties may need support. This may be provided by stretching wire on either side of the hedge row, 3 feet above ground. The wire confines the canes to the hedge row. To make the canes stand erect, it may be necessary to tie the them to the wire with soft twine. Twenty-five feet of row should produce 15 to 20 pounds of raspberries per year.

Berries will form on cane tips the first season after planting. Cut back half the tips after leaves fall in November. Rake or blow away leaves around the plants. This leaf removal will eliminate problems that arise from diseases and over-wintering insects.

There are several raspberry varieties available for deciduous climates: Boyne for mountain areas, and Pathfinder, Newburgh, Canby, Trailblazer, Heritage, September, Fall Red and Fall Gold for lower altitudes. Latham is an old variety no longer widely grown.

Dormant canes secured to wires

Fall-bearing red raspberries recommended for trial include Redwing, August Red. Heritage, Fall Red, Fall Gold (yellow-fruited) and September. My mother, living in Denver, Co., reports that her fall berries start to form buds in August and more times than not, never ripen and are killed by frost.

There are two types of red raspberries, summer-bearing, and fall-bearing. The standard varieties are biennial summer-bearers that produce canes the first season and bear fruit on short lateral branches of these canes the following summer and fall-bearing raspberries, which produce canes (suckers) from the roots but require no dormant period for fruiting. These canes bear fruit in August and September of the first season. These canes may produce a light summer crop, but this is done at the expense of a reduced fall crop.

PRUNING

Some growers advise pruning ever-bearing canes to soil level, after harvesting. The plants will grow from the plant's base and will fruit at the tips in August and September. Cut and remove the canes of summer-bearing varieties. Cut them off at the ground after they bear fruit. Dispose of these canes since they often harbor insects and disease.

WINTER

As a winter protection in colder climates, withhold water after the first frost to help harden off the plants. A late November watering reduces winter desiccation.

After soil is frozen protect plants with evergreen boughs. In dry years, water plants monthly during winter. Remove boughs in late March and rough up the soil to close frost cracks and prepare for moisture absorption from late snows and spring rain.

SPRING

In late April fertilize with 10-6-4 at the rate of one-half cup per plant and and water well. Canes should be thinned each spring to maintain. Leave only the strongest canes for each raspberry "hill".

If you are doing a hedge row remove the dead canes, the weak and small canes as well, leaving no canes closer than six inches apart. Cut off the winter-killed tips of the remaining canes. Some stray canes may come up as far a 6 feet away. Dig them up and give them away; share the wealth. They make welcome gifts for friends.

Apply an inch of water per week early in the season and three inches weekly during flowering and fruiting. A drip system of porous hose is ideal. Put the soaker hoses in place before the blossoms start to form if possible.

Insects and diseases are minimal, but scrutinize those plants early on and take care of problems quickly to guarantee a maximum of healthy fruit.

The plants will bloom in late May and June are perennial, but their life and drama is not simple. Their sweetness is hard won. It is the triumph that tender care brings.

SUMMER

One now faces adversity, the tangle of a rambling raspberry bush. The harvest is not unlike that of cutting roses. Your hands, arms and legs will have scratches that will last longer than the taste of fruit. While the bushes are the rough and tumble in appearance, they are quite fragile and will break at a joint and at the base, with just a bump. The berry itself requires a soft, gentle hand.

Ripeness is all: Picking the berry is simple for even the city slicker if he has a few pointers. An under-ripe berry is pale raspberry pink and decidedly shiny; at the point of perfection it is deeper in color, a true raspberry hue, and no longer shiny but showing a faint "bloom"; overripe, it is dark and dusty-looking. The ripe berry falls into the hand. It comes away from the stem without resisting when surrounded by two fingers and a thumb. The core is left behind on the plant, thus the hole in the berry, which is actually a group of tiny individual fruits, and fits old name "thimbleberry." Overripe berries crumble or squash when you tackle them; pass them by.

PICKING CONTAINERS

Do not pile raspberries high in picking containers—shallow boxes or trays are best, if you are picking for beautiful berries. A tightly woven reed of some variety, basket with a handle, is a good container for jam picking. If you are going to freeze them, consider picking directly into the freezer containers.

Lazy-like picking, where the bucket is carelessly tossed about, results in jam. Whoops!

YIELD

A 25-food hedge row of red raspberries should yield 15 to 20 pounds of fruit per year under optimum conditions. This level of productivity should be reached in the third year. After this productivity will decline. Start with new stock and relocate in 8 to 10 years.

The greatest abundance of raspberries come from your patch, the farm or the market in the month of July. Too many raspberries just cannot be a problem. They freeze well, in the form of sauces, or berries, they make into jams and syrups easily, and if there is a surplus in the kitchen if you leave them where they are visible they will disappear! In this disappearing act one should observe this food for thought: Tom Stobart, in his *The Cook's Encyclopedia* (Harper and Row), said "To get the most of their flavor, it is better to squash them against the roof of the mouth with the tongue than to bite them."

They have such a beautiful, delicate perfume and exquisite flavor all of their own so there is no real need for embellishment. The perfect dessert is of course, perfect raspberries.

When you have a "patch" of your own you will be in touch with their taste and aroma and with this knowledge you will be inspired to try using them in a creative manner coming up with your own new recipes. We know that cooks will forever be creative and look for new ways to gild the lily.

Our forebearers must have grown prodigious amounts of the fruit judging by the quantities of berries called for in older recipes. Raspberry vinegar, sometimes called "shrub", called for steeping, in succession, many large batches of raspberries into a quantity of vinegar. This mixture was finally strained, sweetened, and bottled to be used as a condiment or beverage base. Recipes heaped raspberries between summer pies, not a bad idea, and were lavish in the berry amounts on mousses, whips, Bavarians, jellies and flummeries.

NEW PLEASURES WITH RASPBERRIES

Today we do enjoy our raspberry legacy, and look forward to discovering new pleasures. Many of the recipes in this book do lend themselves to improvisation due to in part to the raspberry's flavor affinities and adaptability. Desserts made with lemon and orange will be improved with raspberry sauce. Do pass the raspberry sauce when serving bread or rice pudding and grate fresh lemon or orange on top.

LIQUEURS AND RASPBERRIES

Many liqueurs are excellent companions: try Raspberry Compote, a bowl of fresh or frozen raspberries pouring gracious amounts of boiling hot sugar syrup, $1/2$ sugar and $1/2$ water. When the compote is cool, add eau-de vie de framboise, cherry or peach brandy, Cream de Cassis, Kirsch, Cointreau or another orange-flavored liqueur; serve it cool, not cold.

How about raspberry butter on croissants, thin cookies, or scones for a special teatime treat. Measure equal amounts of unsalted butter and raspberries and then add half as much confectioners sugar. Beat this up. You will now have a delicate pink butter to serve creatively.

When and if raspberries are scarce, add other fruit. Strawberries, cherries, blackberries and blueberries do well together. Peaches, nectarines and pineapple diced up, sweetened slightly, and adding just a few drops of vanilla, the secret flavor enhancer. To this peachy mixture add the berries. Another exotic combination are figs and raspberries. Scatter raspberries over individual platefuls of sliced ripe figs and pass some sour cream.

PROBLEMS WITH RASPBERRIES

Raspberries are affected by a wide range of diseases and insects, as are most cultivated plants. The gardener can avoid many of the problems for years if only quality, true-to name, disease-free raspberry varieties are purchased.

SYMPTOM

The leaves on some of the plants wilt, then curl, then leaf or leaves turns hard, and has a bluish brown color. It could be Rust or Spider Mites.

RUST

If you have mulched, which is good, it is probable that your brown leaves are the result of "Rust". If raspberries were not edible you would zap this problem with a fungicide. Since we are eating them, an organic spray is appropriate.

Rust Organic Spray
1 teaspoon of baking soda
$1/2$ of a teaspoon of either Ivory dish soap, or any of the dish washing liquids

Mix the ingredients together. Spray the plants in early morning or evening. Do not spray in the heat of the day.

SPIDER MITES

It is almost a given, that during hot, dry weather, raspberries will be infested with spider mites. The mites themselves are not obvious, but if you see tiny yellow spots on the leaves that eventually turn brown, then the spider mites are flourishing. The mites feed on the underside of the leaves.

Leaves look dusty, and or webby. The leaves on some of the plants wilt, then curl, then leaf or leaves turns hard, and has a bluish brown color. Spider mites appear when it is dry.

To check for Spider Mites: The spiders are microscopic, and really hard to discern so try shaking and or rubbing a leaf on a piece of white paper. If there is a dusty residue treat for Spider Mites.

Spider Mite Organic Spray
1 teaspoon of dish soap
1 crushed clove of garlic
1 quart of water

Do not spray in the heat of the day. The herb cure is to plant Coriander between your plants. Coriander is the repellent herb for the Spider Mite.

CANEBORERS

Raspberry cane borers have been reported in many states. They are a serious pest. Their presence is indicated by the sudden wilting and drooping of tops of canes. The white larvae of the borer, if left uncontrolled burrows down through the cane, killing it. Control here is achieved by removing the infected canes at the very beginning of an infestation.

Sevin as well as other insecticides applied before blossoms open will control this insect. Gill Schoonveld, a friend, used to swear that putting down mothballs around the base of the canes, in the spring when the moths are laying their eggs, will ward off the female and thus prevent the larva from getting a start. Now he says "Mothballs work but they are dangerous. Use a commercial spray."

Apply Spider mite spray, the teaspoon of dishwashing detergent and one garlic clove mashes into a quart of water. Do not spray in the heat of the day. Planting garlic or marigolds in and among plants will also repel the borers.

BUYING THEM AT THE MARKET PLACE

There are black, yellow, white, wild and of course red raspberries. The red ones have a dominant place among the raspberries because they are easy to pick and easily transported. No matter what the color is of the berry, make sure if there are any stems at all, that they are a healthy green and the berries are plump, dry, cool to touch and free of any mold.

The beautiful berry is a sure sign of best quality. Buy beauty in raspberries, beauty here is more than skin deep, it's quality. When making your purchase, reject any containers with a lackluster cargo.

Dark-looking, dull berries are over the hill. Overripe ones sink and dwindle fast in the container; when even some of them have done this, the basket isn't worth taking home. Inspect the bottoms of baskets; moisture indicates that some berries have been squashed or perhaps molded. A few moldy berries will spoil all the berries in a container. Containers always have a few crushed berries, so be sure to eat them very soon or make them into a sauce, as they will not keep as long as the whole berries.

A raspberry's sweetness is veiled by a musky, some say bitter, perfume. Authenticity is the lesson here. The fruit is no less sweet because its sweetness is slow to be revealed.

STORING YOUR LITTLE TREASURES

In the best situation possible, raspberries would be eaten at the very moment of their being picked. When in coming upon a wild raspberry patch, simply stand there feasting. Next best is to enjoy them soon after picking, having kept them meanwhile in a cool but not cold place, since they lose their delicate perfume when stored too long or when chilled. If you can't employ this ideal timing, then buy or pick with care and store wisely.

Do you need to wash raspberries?

Raspberries are fragile and must be washed delicately removing the leaves and stems by hand. After picking from our own bushes, we do not, neither do we wash berries from a pick-your-own patch. But if you prefer to wash berries, make the rinse a quick one just before you use them.

You can store them unwashed in the refrigerator for a few days, in shallow, uncovered, dry containers. If you want blue raspberries then put them in iron or aluminum containers. These metals have the ability to turn a happy red into a spooky blue.

At home, refrigerate or turn them onto a plate and then refrigerate. If the plan is to serve them with sugar, add it now. The sugar, plus refrigeration, keeps them in good condition when held for more than a few hours. Raspberries in peak condition will keep at most for two days.

FREEZING

Freezing keeps the nutrition in the berries. They will keep frozen for a year, if you can keep you hands off them, in a freezer that maintains a temperature of 0 degrees or less.

Container/Bag Method: Freeze them after picking them clean. Wash them if you feel the need, by dropping the berries, a few at a time into a bowl of cold water, lift them out gently, and drain them on paper toweling. Handle with care. Next, put them in hard plastic containers or freezer bags. Bags take so little of your storage space.

Tray method: Spread raspberries in a single layer on jelly-roll pans and slip into the freezer until hard, usually an hour or two. Transfer the fruit to rigid freezers or heavy-duty freezer bags; seal, expelling all possible air, label, and return to the freezer.

SUGARLESS PACK

Place berries gently in rigid freezer containers, shake lightly to settle them, cover, expel air, seal, label, and freeze. Heavy plastic bags can also be used, but do not pile them in the freezer until the berries are hard.

WITH SUGAR

Stir berries very gently with sugar on a wide platter, using rubber spatula and allowing 3/4 cup superfine sugar to a quart. Let stand until the sugar partly dissolves, then pack, cover, expel air, seal, label and freeze.

WITH SYRUP

Make a medium, 50% syrup of 2-1/2 cups of sugar to each 2 cups water, chill. Pack berries in rigid containers, leaving 1/2 inch head-space for pints 3/4 to one inch for quarts. Cover berries with syrup, cover, expel air, seal, label and freeze.

DRYING RASPBERRIES

Dried raspberries need to be rehydrated or ground to use. Raspberries and all the other berries make a fine fruit leather. The berries for drying should look bright and fresh, not overripe or soft.

To prepare them simply dry whole and if very large cut them in half. They need 10 to 16 hours of drying time in a dehydrator. The berries when sufficiently dry will be hard and crisp.

CANNING

Place the berries in colander that sets down in a deep pan full of cold water. Lift colander up and down to wash but not to crush the berries. Remove stems. Prepare syrup.

Syrup consists of 1 quart of water with 1 cup of sugar or honey. This syrup must be boiled before adding it to the fruit. Pack the berries in hot sterilized jars, pour in the boiling syrup, leave 1/2 to 1 inch space at the top of the jar. Place jars on rack of boiler, with warm water to cover.

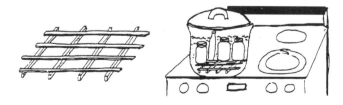

Boil at 212 degrees F. in a water bath for six minutes. Remove jars, place on folded towel, seal at once, tightly, with self seal rubbers. Cool upright out of drafts.

REMOVING RASPBERRY STAINS

The suggestions below apply to linen, cotton and wool. For acrylic, acetates and rayon follow manufacturer's directions. Stretch the stained part over a bowl, and pour boiling water through it from a height of 12" or more until the stain disappears. If stain remains, hang material in the sun to dry.

When possible remove all stains while they are fresh, like immediately. If a stain has been overlooked and washed in, it is difficult to remove and should be bleached with a commercial bleach and/or put in the sun for natural bleaching.

FAT REDUCING SUBSTITUTES

So many people these days must watch their fat intake. I try to do this in most of the recipes in the book. If you have a need to cut further here are some easy delicious, nutritious, substitute ingredients, which can be used in putting together desserts and breads. A good way to begin is to reduce just half of the recipe. Evaluate results and then reduce further next time. If your end product is tough then add a tablespoon or two of lecithin granules.

Lecithin is a soybean oil by product which is both nutritious, and an enhancer for the texture of fat-free baked goods. It is used in some of the recipes to allow batters to rise more and achieve a softer texture to the final product. For example a bundt cake could contain 1-$\frac{1}{2}$ tablespoons of lecithin to improve its texture. The best granules to use are those finely ground. They contain vitamin E, iron, calcium, choline, and phosphorus. Lecithin liquid and granules can be purchased at health food stores. Either form needs to be refrigerated to maintain freshness.

Bananas to replace butter, margarine or oil in recipes. You gain nutritionally too. Just the potassium alone gained from using bananas, makes this fat substitute worth while. When the pie crust calls for $\frac{1}{2}$ cup shortening, or oil replace it with the same amount, $\frac{1}{2}$ cup of mashed bananas. If your bananas are on the real ripe side, freeze them and then unthaw and use later. It really works! Bananas work well in muffins, quick breads and chocolate cake.

Applesauce to replace fat works for recipes in which you do not want to change the original flavor. Squash and sweet potato can replace all fat in cakes, breads and cookies.

Prunes will reduce the fat and boost the nutrition in all recipes where fruit is a main ingredient in the baked goods. Prunes have high content of fiber and carbohydrates and hold moisture. Just $\frac{1}{4}$ cup of puree contains 39 calories and can replace $\frac{1}{2}$ cup of margarine or butter containing 810 calories, or oil 950 calories! The other factor here is that when replacing with prunes you replace a high-fat ingredient with a no fat ingredient. Use equal amounts of Prune Butter to replace all or part of the butter or margarine in crumb toppings. Reduce sugar by one-half to two-thirds by using the same amount of Prune Butter in a recipe.

Prune Puree and Prune Butter reduce the fat, and sugar but add nutrition and fiber. You can make them ahead and have them on hand when it is time to bake or make sweets. While you cannot buy Prune Puree or Butter in stores, you can buy baby food prunes and it is easily made at home.

PUREE

1/2 cup or 3 ounces of pitted prunes, 1 cup water or fruit juice, 2 teaspoons lecithin granules, placed in a blender until smooth. Put 1-1/2 cups of puree into an airtight container and store. It will keep up to 4 weeks in the refrigerator.

BUTTER

1-1/3 cups or 8 ounces pitted prunes and 6 tablespoons of water or fruit juice placed in a food processor. Process at high until there is a smooth paste. Use procedure above to store.

Reduced-fat, *lite* margarine and *lite* butter can be used for baking and reduce fat significantly.

Substituting dairy fat with nonfat yogurt and nonfat buttermilk can replace all of the fat in cakes, muffins, quick breads and at least half of the fat in cookies.

Salt: Sodium and chloride or salt enhances the flavors of many foods. A little salt added to cookie, cake or other dessert recipe can reduce the need for sugar. For this reason, some of the recipes in this book call for a small amount of salt as an optional.

Egg whites are fat-free, and many of the book recipes call for them. Why would one of these ingredients be listed instead of the other? Most often the two ingredients can be used interchangeably. Recipes that ask for whipped egg whites, egg substitutes simply don't work; the exception rather than the rule.

If you are using fresh eggs and feel throwing out yolks is wasteful, substitute two large whole eggs for three egg whites in any recipe. Keep in mind that two large eggs will add 10 grams of fat and 420 milligrams of cholesterol to the recipe. The latest news is that whole eggs are ok.

Here are some egg guidelines:

1 large egg= 1-1/2 large egg whites

1 large egg= 3 tablespoons egg substitute

1 large egg white= 2 tablespoons egg substitute

MENU COMBINATIONS FOR SPECIAL OCCASIONS

We all value the well thought out and prepared meals. Start with the freshest and best of foods. Serve the meal well, think about the best and most appealing presentation. Take time to pause, gain nutrition, enjoy the raspberries, food and the company.

THE RELAXED RASPBERRY BRUNCH
Raspberry Smoothie
Dutch Babies served with Melba Sauce
Turkey bacon
Pero or Coffee

A SUMMER RASPBERRY CELEBRATION
Raspberry Cordial
Chilled Raspberry Soup
Raspberry Tomato Salad Mold
Pan Seared Duck with Raspberry Sauce
Rice pilaf
Chocolate Hazelnut Ricotta Mousse Cake
Coffee or Heath and Heather Raspberry Tea

PICNIC RASPBERRY FARE
Raspberry May Wine
Wild Vegetation Salad
Trout with Raspberry Fish Sauce
Raspberry Up-Side-Down Cake
Raspberry-Mint Tea Cooler

A WINTER RASPBERRY REMINDER MEAL
A Chambord Cocktail
Raspberry Orange Soup
Rich Raspberry Spinach Salad
Raspberry Chicken with Raspberry Yams
Raspberry Cheesecake Pie
Coffee and Raspberry Tea

RASPBERRY CORDIAL

The basic directions apply to either recipe for cordial.

1 pint fresh raspberries, or equivalent in frozen dry-packed
2-1/2 cups good quality vodka
1 vanilla bean, cut into 1-inch pieces
1/2 teaspoon peppercorns, bruised
1/4 teaspoon whole allspice, bruised
1/2 cup light corn syrup

1. Crush the berries roughly in a bowl. Scrape into a 1-quart widemouthed canning jar or any widemouthed container that closes tightly. Add the vodka, vanilla, peppercorns and allspice. Cover tightly and shake well.
2. Let stand from seven to ten days. Shake the container heartily whenever you pass by.
3. Strain the liqueur, a small batch at a time, through a layer of damp fine mesh cheese cloth. Press down lightly on the berries to extract the juice, and discard the solids.
4. Rinse the cloth and fold it to form 2 to 3 layers. Strain the cordial through this and add the corn syrup to taste. Pour into a bottle that does not allow much airspace and store for months.

THE BASE:

Choose a moderately priced spirit. No amount of fruit can sufficiently cover up the taste of harsh cheap firewater. Similarly, avoid the most expensive liqueurs since the subtle and costly complexities of well-aged brandy, for example, will undoubtedly be masked if not lost by the other ingredients.

PROCEDURE:

A ratio of one quart of fruit per one fifth of alcohol (four-fifths of a quart) is appropriate. Wash and dry the fruit and mash it gently to release its flavor. Put it in a widemouthed jar, cover with alcohol and store in a cool dark spot to age.

The difficult part is the wait. You must wait for a good taste from one to three months, and you must taste and shake this mixture periodically. This chore can be made more fun if you do it with a friend. This friend can also give you their input on taste and you know, two heads are always better than one. When you are pleased with the strength of the fruit flavor, strain the mixture through a funnel lined with coffee filter paper. This will result in a clearer, prettier product.

To sweeten, make a simple sugar syrup by boiling equal parts of water and sugar for five minutes. Allow to cool and add, a few tablespoons at a time, to the strained cordial until the desired degree of sweetness is achieved. One or two cups of syrup will flavor a fifth of alcohol.

Rebottle in decanters or in the unusual liquor bottles that you have saved for this purpose. When served in tiny glasses or splashed on a dish of vanilla ice cream, home-made cordials are an elegant finale to a special dinner. And if you can bring yourself to part with them, they make wonderful, sure-to-please presents.

Yield: 3 cups

EASY RASPBERRY CORDIAL

Quick-easy Raspberry Cordial Cordially yours for a simple version of this ruby delicious treat, that will save the essence of fresh raspberries to taste in the cold winter months.

1 quart raspberries
1 quart vodka
1 pound sugar

Combine raspberries, vodka, and sugar and stir well. Store in a dark, cool place for about 6 weeks. Turn or rotate daily. Filter and bottle. Store in a dark, cool place.

RASPBERRY SEASON DAIQUIRI

4 cups fresh or frozen raspberries
1/3 to 1/2 cup sugar
6 -ounce can frozen lemonade concentrate
4 cups crushed ice
1 cup light rum

Combine raspberries with sugar, lemonade, ice and rum in blender. Whirl until smooth. Spoon into large glasses and serve immediately.

RASPBERRY MAY WINE

A celebration of spring. This is a special treat when the white flowers of the woodruff are blossoming. Plant some sweet woodruff and start your own tradition.

3 litters Rhine wine
1/2 cup sweet woodruff, new growth
1 orange, sliced
1 lemon, sliced
1 cup raspberries

Combine the wine, sweet woodruff and raspberries. Serve in a big punch bowl in the backyard while your guests enjoy the woodruffed scented air.

FRUITED RASPBERRY PUNCH

1 10-ounce package frozen red raspberries
1 8-ounce can crushed pineapple, chilled
1 12-ounce can frozen lemonade concentrate, thawed, with water added
2 quarts lemon-lime carbonated beverage, chilled

In a blender container combine raspberries and pineapple. Cover and blend until smooth. Pour into punch bowl. Stir in lemonade concentrate. Slowly add carbonated beverage.

RASPBERRY FIZZ

A raspberry refresher. When the sun is hot and high in the sky, sit in your lawn chair and enjoy the essence of summer.

6 ounces frozen orangeade concentrate
6 ounces rum or tequila
1 tablespoon Rose's lime juice
2 cups fresh or frozen raspberries
2-3 cups (about 14) ice cubes
Fresh orange slices for garnishing

In blender, combine above ingredients in order written. Process until smooth. Serve in chilled glasses garnished with orange slices.

Yield: *4 portions*

RASPBERRY SMOOTHIE

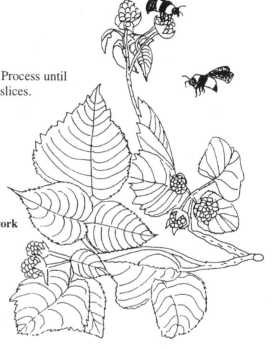

A nutritious, cool, summer's specialty drink for all the family.

1 cup fruit flavored yogurt (raspberry, peach, or orange work
  best) or 1 cup Alta Dena Nonfat liquid yogurt
1 cup orange juice
1 pealed peach or mango
1 cup crushed ice
¹/₂ cup raspberries

Combine above ingredients in the blender. Process until smooth. Serve in chilled glasses.

Yield: *10 (8-ounce) servings*

ORANGE BERRY COOLERS

2 cups strawberries, hulled
2 cups raspberries, picked over
2 ¹/₂ cups fresh orange juice
¹/₂ cup superfine sugar plus additional to taste
1 tablespoon fresh lime juice, or to taste
Seltzer or club soda

In a blender blend berries, orange juice, ¹/₂ cup sugar, and lime juice until smooth. Force puree through a fine sieve into a large measuring cup or bowl, pressing hard on solids. Chill puree, covered, until cold. Stir in additional sugar. Puree keeps for 2 days if covered and chilled.

Fill tall glasses with ice and add enough berry puree to fill each glass by three quarters. Top off drinks with seltzer or club soda and stir well.

Yield: *about 5 cups berry puree*

RASPBERRIES SUNRISE SHAKE

Breakfast does not get any easier than this. Encourage kids to make their own shakes - a great way to introduce them to basic cooking skills (and tofu). This shake only takes 5 minutes to prepare, which is another plus.

1 10.5-ounce box silken tofu
1 cup fresh raspberries
$^1/_2$ cup orange juice
1 tablespoon honey or rice syrup
2 tablespoons fresh lemon or lime juice
1 cup ice cubes

Puree all the ingredients in a blender until creamy smooth.

Yield: 4 cups

RASPBERRY MINT TEA COOLER

1-$^1/_3$ cups tea concentrate (recipe follows)
1 cup firmly packed mint leaves
2-$^1/_3$ cups chilled sparkling water
$^1/_2$ cup frozen raspberry juice concentrate
$^1/_2$ cup half and half, whipping cream or non-fat vanilla yogurt
Ice cubes

In a 1-$^1/_2$ quart pan, combine tea concentrate and mint; bring to boil. Cover, chill until cold, at least 1 hour or up to 2 days. Pour concentrate through a fine strainer into a pitcher; add sparkling water. Discard mint.

Fill 4 tall glasses (12 oz. or larger) with ice cubes. To layer drink, pour raspberry concentrate equally into each glass, and gently fill glasses with the tea mixture. Stir beverage to mix as you sip.

Yield: Makes 4 servings

TEA CONCENTRATE

Combine $^1/_4$ cup loose tea leaves or 12 tea bags (any flavor or variety) with 5 cups water in a 3-4 quart pan. Bring to boil; boil, uncovered, until liquid is reduced to 4 cups, about 6 minutes. Pour liquid through a fine strainer if using loose tea. Cover and chill at least 3 hours or up to 2 weeks.

Yield: Makes 12 servings when diluted

RASPBERRY JUICE WITH OPTIONS

This juice can be prepared using a food processor or a domestic juicer to pulp the raspberries plant. Squeeze the pulp through a nylon sieve or jelly bag to obtain juice. Large quantities of berries are needed. Example: 6 cups of berries will yield 2 cups of juice. You can add either apple, orange or cranberry juice to extend the raspberry juice.

Summery Soups and Salads Using Cool Raspberries

Raspberries have a delightfully powerful flavor, so they can make soup a more versatile experience. One can serve raspberry soup at the beginning or end of a meal.

The following salad recipes have raspberries in combination with fancy mixed greens, crumbled mild goat cheese, slivers of Belgian endive, and very thin slices of sweet red and yellow pepper. These salads can be flavored with poppy seed raspberry dressing or balsamic vinegar, Dijon mustard dressing. Chunks of chicken, thin slices of roast beef, or seasoned, baked tofu, are additions that make these salads perfect for a summer entree.

REFRESHING RASPBERRY SOUP

1-1/2 tablespoons unflavored gelatin
1/3 cup cold water
3/4 cup hot water
3 cups fresh or thawed raspberries
3-1/2 cups non-fat vanilla yogurt
1-1/3 cups pineapple juice
1 cup non-fat sour cream
1 cup peach or apricot brandy
Garnishes: mint or and or whole raspberries

Soak gelatin in cold water for 5 minutes. Stir in hot water and dissolve over low heat. Push raspberries through a strainer to remove seeds, then puree. Combine all ingredients and place in a glass bowl. Cover and refrigerate 2 to 3 hours or over-night. Garnish with mint and or fresh raspberries

Tip: Perfect served as a first course for a luncheon. Left-over soup can be frozen for a yogurt-like snack or frozen into *Dream Bars.*

ORANGE-RASPBERRY SOUP

2 cups light cream or half and half or non-fat yogurt
1 package(10-ounce) frozen raspberries, thawed
1 can (6-ounce) frozen concentrated orange juice, thawed, undiluted
1/2 cup heavy cream, whipped
Mandarin orange slices and fresh raspberries
Grated orange rind

In an electric blender combine light cream, raspberries and concentrated orange juice. Cover. Process on high one minute until smooth. Chill. Garnish with whipped cream or, for non-fat alternative, garnish with fresh raspberries, mandarin orange slices and slivered almonds. Sprinkle with grated orange rind, if desired.

Yield: 4 servings; about 5 cups

COLORADO RASPBERRY SOUP

1 cup raspberries
¹/₂ cup sour cream
1 cup rose wine
¹/₂ cup brown sugar

Combine in blender or food processor until smooth. Chill overnight. Serve cold.

Yield: 6-1/2 cup servings

RASPBERRY WINE DESSERT SOUP

A lively fruit soup made with rose wine, to be chilled and served as dessert with a tuft of sour cream and a few sole raspberries atop each helping. The soup is not overly sweet, so it would be equally welcome as a luncheon starter on a hot day.

3-¹/₂ cups fresh raspberries, picked over, rinsed and drained if necessary
³/₄ cup plus 2 tablespoons water
2 tablespoons finely chopped (not grated) orange zest
2 tablespoons cornstarch
Pinch of salt
³/₄ cup sugar
2 cups rose wine, preferably Anjou
Sour cream or substitute with non-fat sour cream

1. Set ¹/₂ cup of raspberries aside for garnish. Puree remainder in blender or food processor; place in medium-mesh sieve set over bowl. Press puree through sieve with back of large spoon; reserve in bowl. Spoon seeds left in sieve into small saucepan.

2. Stir the ³/₄ cup water into seeds in saucepan; add orange zest. Heat over medium heat to simmering. Reduce heat to low; simmer, covered, 5 minutes. Strain mixture into small bowl; discard seeds. Return liquid to saucepan.

3. Stir together cornstarch and the 2 tablespoons water in small bowl until smooth; stir into liquid in saucepan until well blended. Heat mixture over low heat, stirring constantly until thickened, about 3 minutes. Stir in salt and sugar until dissolved; stir in raspberry puree and wine until well blended.

4. Refrigerate soup, covered, until well chilled, about 2 hours. Serve in chilled dessert bowls, each portion garnished with a spoonful of sour cream (yogurt) and a few of the reserved whole raspberries.

Yield: Makes 6 ³/₄ cup servings

ROCKY MOUNTAIN FRUIT SOUP

$1/_2$ pound fresh raspberries, strawberries, blueberries, or blackberries
1 quart water
1 tablespoon tapioca
$1/_4$ cup cold water
1 tablespoon lemon juice
2 tablespoons sugar
$1/_4$ cup white wine
Garnish: Whipped cream or non-fat yogurt

Reserve a few whole ripe berries. Cook the rest of the berries in water until soft. Drain and reserve juice. Puree the cooked fruit briefly in a blender or food processor, adding a small amount of juice as needed. Dissolve tapioca in cold water and add to berry liquid. Mix together juice and sugar to taste. Allow to cool. Stir in white wine. Garnish each bowl with a few ripe berries and a spoonful of whipped cream.

Yield: *8 portions*

RASPBERRY-CHAMPAGNE SOUP

$1/_2$ cup sugar
$1/_2$ cup water
1-$1/_2$ pints fresh raspberries
2 cups good quality Champagne or other sparkling wine, chilled
1 pint Berry Sorbet, page 71

Combine the sugar and water in a small saucepan over medium heat. Simmer just enough until the sugar dissolves. Let cool. Place all but one-half cup of the raspberries in a blender with the sugar syrup. Puree until smooth. Strain through a fine mesh sieve and refrigerate until cold. Just before serving, divide the soup mixture among four bowls and add one-half cup of Champagne to each. Place a scoop of sorbet in the soup and garnish with the remaining raspberries.

Yield: *4 servings*

BIBB LETTUCE & RASPBERRIES

1 head bibb lettuce
1 cup fresh raspberries
$1/_2$ cup mandarin oranges or dried apricots
$1/_2$ cup pecans

Combine lettuce, raspberries and oranges. In a separate bowl combine $3/4$ cup olive oil, $1/4$ cup raspberry vinegar. Add sugar, salt and pepper to taste. Stir well and pour over the salad. Sprinkle pecans over the top.

RASPBERRY RED & GREEN SALAD

VINAIGRETTE
4 -1/2 teaspoons Dijon mustard
4 tablespoons balsamic vinegar
5 tablespoons olive oil
Sea salt and freshly ground pepper, to taste

In a small mixing bowl place the mustard and whisk in the vinegar. Whisk in the olive oil. This mixture will thicken as the mustard combines with the oil. Set this mixture aside after you season it with salt and pepper.

RASPBERRY POPPY SEED DRESSING

To one cup of Raspberry Vinegar (page 31) add 2 tablespoons of olive oil, and 2 tablespoons of poppy seeds. For a fat-free dressing, replace olive oil with water. Whisk this mixture to combine ingredients.

These dressings can be made several hours ahead and stored with a cover, in the refrigerator. The dressing needs to be taken out of the refrigerator several hours before using it, to facilitate tossing and pouring.

SALAD
1 head of Belgian endive, or 1 head of butter lettuce, leaves separated, washed and dried
9 cups of mixed greens, also washed and dried
1 avocado halved, cut in small squares and set aside
3/4 cup of yellow and or red pepper, seeded and cut into tiny match sticks

Cut lettuce or endive leaves diagonally in approximately 1/2 inch slices. Drizzle the dressing over, toss. Spread avocado slices over tossed leaves.

TOPPINGS
5 red onion slices, separated into thin rings
7 tablespoons crumbled goat cheese (2-3 ounces)
2 cups of chicken, turkey, thinly sliced rare roast beef, or seasoned, baked tofu
3/4 cup fresh raspberries

Divide the greens among 6 chilled plates. Arrange the raspberries, protein choice, cheese and onion slices on top the avocado, lettuce mixture.

Yield: Makes 6 servings

SPINACH SALAD WITH GRILLED CHICKEN, MANGO & RASPBERRIES

This is the ideal one meal, light summer salad. Serve in a buffet for company with raspberry muffins and a raspberry sorbet dessert.

DRESSING

2 tablespoons raspberry vinegar
1 tablespoon balsamic vinegar
1 tablespoon soy sauce
$3/4$ teaspoon Dijon mustard
1-$1/2$ teaspoons minced fresh ginger root
1 garlic clove, minced with $1/4$ teaspoon chili powder
$1/4$ teaspoon freshly ground black pepper, or to taste
$1/3$ cup extra-virgin olive oil

SALAD INGREDIENTS

1 whole skinless boneless chicken breast (about $3/4$ pound), halved
1 bunch spinach (about $3/4$ pound), coarse stems discarded with leaves washed well and spun dry
1 firm-ripe mango, cut into $1/4$-inch thick slices
2 plum tomatoes, sliced thin
$2/3$ cup raspberries, picked over
4 scallions, chopped fine
$1/4$ cup walnuts, toasted and chopped coarse

1. To make the dressing, whisk together all ingredients except oil. Add oil in a stream, constantly whisking mixture. Dressing may be made 2 days ahead and chilled, covered.
2. To make the chicken, coat chicken with 3 tablespoons dressing. Marinate, covered and chilled, for 2 hours in a shallow dish or resealable plastic bag.
3. Heat an oiled well-seasoned ridged grill pan but not smoking. Grill chicken, until cooked through, about 7 minutes on each side. Transfer chicken to a platter and cool. Chicken can be prepared 1 day ahead, then chilled and covered.
4. Cut chicken into $1/4$-inch thick slices and in a large bowl combine with remaining ingredients. Drizzle remaining dressing over salad and toss gently to combine.

Yield: Serves 4 generously

RASPBERRY-RICH SPINACH SALAD

This outstanding salad delights the palate and excites the eye. Equally as splendid with strawberries.

2 tablespoons raspberry vinegar
2 tablespoons raspberry jam
1/3 cup vegetable oil
8 cups spinach, rinsed, stemmed and torn into pieces
3/4 cup coarsely shopped macadamia nuts
1 cup fresh raspberries
3 kiwis, peeled and sliced

To prepare dressing, combine vinegar and jam in blender or small bowl. Add oil in a thin stream, blending well. Toss spinach, 1/2 of raspberries and 1/2 of kiwis with dressing on a platter or in a salad bowl. Top with remaining nuts, raspberries and kiwis. Serve immediately.

RAZZELDAZZLE SPINACH SALAD

The raspberries and tender spinach are complement ingredients in this refreshing salad. Top it off with the Raspberry-Poppy Seed Vinaigrette salad dressing and if you want it as a main course, add slices or chicken or turkey.

1 pound of tender spinach or equal amounts of young dandelion greens, washed and stems removed
2 cups raspberries
1 yellow pepper, sliced in rings
1/4 cup pecan halves

DRESSING

1 tablespoon olive oil
1/2 cup fresh orange juice
1/4 cup champagne, raspberry, or white wine vinegar
2 teaspoons honey or rice syrup
1/2 teaspoon dry mustard
1/2 teaspoon poppy seeds

Combine olive oil, orange juice, vinegar, honey, poppy seeds and mustard in a jar with a tight lid and shake well. Divide greens, raspberries, yellow pepper rings and pecans among your 4-5 salad plates. Garnish with edible pesticide-free flowers, such as pansies or nasturtiums. Serve dressing on the side.

Yield: Serves 4-5

RASPBERRY TOMATO SALAD MOLD

Here is another jello salad that is magnificent in red color. If made in a special, lovely or dramatic 2-quart ring mold and then unmolded onto a bed of greens such as raspberry leaves, watercress, mint, or parsley.

3 boxes (3-ounces each) raspberry gelatin
3/4 to 1 cup hot water
3 cans (16-ounce each) stewed tomatoes
2 to 4 dashes Tabasco (or to taste)
Sour cream in desired quantity
Horseradish to taste

Dissolve gelatin in hot water. Mix in stewed tomatoes and Tabasco. Pour into 2 quart mold and refrigerate until set. Mix sour cream and horseradish. Unmold salad and serve with dressing.

Yield: 8-12 servings

RASPBERRY MANDARIN SALAD

As always the raspberry and any kind of citrus fruit make very nice companions. This salad then is made better by the raspberry touch. The fruity raspberry vinaigrette dressing is a good match on this salad as well as the dressing shown on this page.

SALAD
1/2 cup sliced almonds
3 tablespoons sugar
1/2 head iceberg lettuce
2 cups spinach
1 cup fresh raspberries or 1 cup frozen thawed raspberries
1 11-ounce can mandarin oranges, drained

DRESSING
1/2 teaspoon salt (optional)
dash pepper
2 whole green onions, chopped
1/4 cup vegetable (olive) oil
1/4 cup raspberry vinegar
2 tablespoons poppy seeds
Dash of Tabasco sauce

In a small pan over medium heat, cook almonds and sugar, stirring constantly until almonds are coated and sugar dissolved. They burn easily so be watchful. Cool and store in an air-tight container, in the refrigerator. Mix all the dressing ingredients and chill. Mix greens. Just before you serve the salad, add the oranges and the raspberries. Toss the salad with dressing.

BLOSSOM-TIME SALAD

This salad is a visual statement about summertime. Luscious and elegant seasonal fruits mixed with pesticide-free flowers are the combination ingredients. You can purchase these ingredients in natural food stores, but not always in the amount and variety that you want, so here again is the motivation to have your own "Patch" of berries and edible flowers.

1 cantaloupe
1 mango or 2 red plums
1 cup blueberries
1 cup raspberries
$^1/_3$ cup strawberries, sliced
1 cup nonfat plain yogurt
$^1/_4$ cup concentrated orange juice
1 tablespoons lime juice
1 tablespoon honey
$^1/_4$ teaspoon vanilla extract
$^1/_4$ teaspoon cinnamon
Pinch lemon or orange zest
1 head washed Bibb lettuce
$^1/_2$ cup tender dandelion greens*
$^1/_2$ cup colorful flower petals, reserve 5 or 6 whole flowers for an artistic touch**

Scoop out the cantaloupe flesh with a melon ball scoop. Slice the mango or plums in crescents after removing pits. Combine all the fruits. Blend all the juices, and yogurt together with the spices and honey for the dressing. Divide the "greens" between 4 or 5 plates. Layer the fruit, then the dressing. Garnish with petals and whole flowers.

* Your "greens" can vary, examples being, spinach, kale, red leaf lettuce, escarole, etc., but do use young and tender varieties. ** Edible flowers include pansy, violet, nasturtium, marigold, lily, purple cone flower (echinacea purpurea) and carnations. (Nasturtiums are quite spicy; they taste like radishes.)

Yield: 4-6 servings

RASPBERRIES FRUIT SALAD

1 package raspberry jello
1 cup boiling water
1-$^1/_2$ cups crushed pineapple
1 small package cream cheese
$^1/_4$ cup canola mayonnaise
1 sliced banana
$^3/_4$ cup shredded coconut
1 cup stiffly whipped cream or yogurt

Dissolve package raspberry jello in boiling water. Add crushed pineapple. Blend the cream cheese and canola oil. Add cream cheese mixture, banana and coconut to the partially set jello. Fold in whipped cream or yogurt. This can be served alone or with your favorite fruit dressing.

ORANGE SLICES WITH WARM RASPBERRIES

Warming the berries enhances their flavor and makes a pleasing contrast to the cool orange slices. Fresh pineapple can stand in for the oranges. This recipe can be used as a salad or dessert.

4 seedless oranges, such as navel oranges
2 tablespoons sugar
1 tablespoon fresh lemon juice
$\frac{1}{4}$ teaspoon ground cinnamon
2 cups frozen unsweetened raspberries (not thawed)

With a sharp knife; remove and discard the skin and white pith from oranges; slice the oranges cross-wise and arrange on 4 dessert plates. In a small saucepan, combine sugar, lemon juice and cinnamon; stir over low heat until bubbling. Add raspberries and stir gently until the berries are just thawed. Spoon over the orange slices and serve immediately.

Yield: Serves 4

SUMMER'S BEST FRUIT SALAD

Creativity and palate reign here, so use your experienced taster and begin using 2 cups of varied fruits such as:

Raspberries
Blueberries
Pears
Peaches
Cantaloupe
Apricots
Kiwi fruit
Strawberries
Mango or papaya cut in squares

DRESSING

2 tablespoons honey
2 tablespoons lemon or lime juice freshly squeezed
2 tablespoons orange liqueur or dark rum

In a jar combine honey, lime juice and liqueur, and shake well. Pour the dressing over the fruit and chill for several hours before serving.

Yield: 4-5 servings

WILD VEGETATION SALAD

This salad is perfect for a camping trip. You can adjust this to fit your mountains or meadows and the month in summer that you attempt it.

Wild vegetation peaks in late July and early August in Colorado. Send out a foraging party. Make it a treasure hunt with colored pictures and a guide with accurate pictures of the plants and flowers.

Dandelion, the young tender leaves
Wild mint
Sheperd's purse
Lambs quarters
Wild onion
Chickweed
Wild raspberries, strawberries
Wood sorrel
Wild mustard

RASPBERRY DRESSING

$1/_4$ cup fresh mint
1 egg (optional)
$1/_2$ cup raspberry vinegar
$3/_4$ cup extra virgin olive oil
Dash salt (optional)
Dash white pepper

Fireweed
unopened buds,
young leaves

Shepherds Purse

Make the dressing ahead, at home, using a blender. Clean the greens. Toss or drizzle the dressing and garnish with pesticide free flowers. Edible flowers include pansy, violas, nasturtium, marigold, lily, purple cone flower (echinacea purpurea), carnations and wild mustard blossoms. (Nasturtiums are quite spicy; taste like radishes.)

RASPBERRY-APPLESAUCE SALAD

This is a favorite of my grandchildren. It is so easy that they help make it.

3 ounce package raspberry jello, or 1 package Knox Gelatin
$1/_4$ cup lemon juice
$1/_2$ cup sugar
1 cup boiling water
10 ounce package frozen raspberries
1 cup applesauce
1 cup non-fat sour cream
1 cup tiny marshmallows
Mixed baby greens or alfalfa sprouts

Softened jello or gelatin mix in lemon juice, then add sugar. Dissolve jello mixture in boiling water. Add slightly thawed raspberries and stir until thawed. Stir in applesauce. Pour into 10 x16 inch pan. Chill until set. Combine non-fat sour cream and marshmallows and spread atop gelatin. Cover and chill 1-2 hours. Serve on mixed baby greens or alfalfa sprouts.

Yield: 10 servings

RASPBERRY VINEGAR

This is delicious recipe for raspberry vinegar. To help save time in separating the juice from the pulp, my aunts used to put the pulp in a cheese cloth and let the pulp hang overnight, allowing it to drip into a container. If you are straining a large amount of berries, this set up would be worth while.

6 cups raspberries
1-1/3 cups wine vinegar
1-1/2 cups sugar

1. Pour the vinegar over the raspberries, gently mix until all the raspberries have been coated with vinegar. Let this mixture stand in a cool place for 20 hours (can be refrigerated for 24 hours). Wash and sterilize jars or bottles, and the corks to stop the tops of the bottles.
2. Strain the juice off the raspberry mixture, use a cheese cloth bag or one could use a food strainer to remove pulp. You should get approximately 3 cups of juice.
3. Add the sugar to the juice. This is the time to taste. If this vinegar is too sweet for you add more vinegar. Bring this mixture to a boil for 10 minutes. For a variation, add 1/2 cup of Peach Schnapps to the mixture after it has boiled the 10 minutes.
4. Using a small funnel pour the vinegar into the sterilized bottles, add the corks and let the mixture in bottles cool.
5. When the filled bottles are cool, seal the corks with wax. Heat wax, (old candles work, cut off dirty wicks) in a tin can or metal container and let the melted wax set for 5-10 minutes. Dip the corked bottle tops in wax.

Yield: 3 cups or enough to fill three 8 ounce bottles

RASPBERRY-POPPY SEED DRESSING

This is the perfect dressing for fruit salads. To one of the bottles of above vinegar just add:

1 tablespoon onion juice
1 tablespoon poppy seed
3/4 tablespoon dry mustard
1/2 cup sugar

Mix sugar, mustard, salt and vinegar in mixer. Add onion juice and stir. Add oil slowly, beating constantly until thick. Add seeds, beat a few minutes.

RASPBERRY-BLUEBERRY VINEGAR

1/4 cup raspberries
1/4 cup blueberries
1-1/2 cups light red wine vinegar

Crush berries through a food mill, blender, or chop coarsely in food processor. Transfer to a bowl and blend in vinegar. Cover and let stand for several days in the refrigerator. Strain and bottle. Keep refrigerated. Excellent served over breast of chicken or duck.

RASPBERRY WINE VINEGAR

2 cups fresh ripe raspberries
2 cups white wine vinegar

Pour vinegar over fruit in a large glass jar. Metal lids cause a reaction with the vinegar, so cover with plastic inside a lid or with a glass plate. Let stand for two to three weeks in a cool dark place. Strain well, heat but do not boil. Pour into clean glass bottles. Close tightly. Seal. If your berries are not sweet enough, a small amount of sugar may be added.

RASPBERRY VINAIGRETTE

Pureed berries thicken this beautiful rose-colored dressing. It's a perfect accent for fresh spinach or peppery greens, avocados or sliced fruit.

1 tea bag, preferably Earl Grey
1/2 cup frozen unsweetened raspberries (not thawed)
1 shallot, peeled and coarsely chopped
1 tablespoon olive oil, preferably extra-virgin
1 tablespoon red wine vinegar
1 teaspoon sugar
1/4 teaspoon salt or to taste
1/4 teaspoon freshly ground black pepper

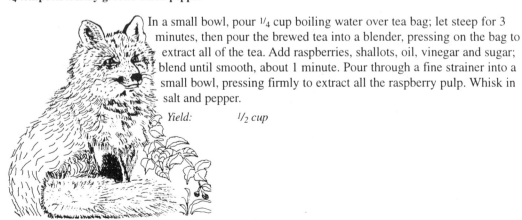

In a small bowl, pour 1/4 cup boiling water over tea bag; let steep for 3 minutes, then pour the brewed tea into a blender, pressing on the bag to extract all of the tea. Add raspberries, shallots, oil, vinegar and sugar; blend until smooth, about 1 minute. Pour through a fine strainer into a small bowl, pressing firmly to extract all the raspberry pulp. Whisk in salt and pepper.

Yield: *1/2 cup*

EASY RASPBERRY VINAIGRETTE

5 tablespoons raspberry vinegar
1/4 cup canola oil
1/4 cup water
2 tablespoons frozen unsweetened raspberries, thawed
1 tablespoon minced shallots
1-1/2 teaspoons sesame oil
1/4 teaspoon salt (optional)
1/4 teaspoon freshly ground black pepper
Dash hot pepper sauce

Add the ingredients to a jar, cover the jar, and shake it to combine the ingredients thoroughly. Chill the dressing for at least 1 hour before using it.

RASPBERRY-TARRAGON VINEGAR

1 17-ounce bottle good quality white-wine vinegar
1 pint fresh raspberries
1/4 cup fresh tarragon leaves and stems, bruised slightly
1 tablespoon honey

Place the vinegar in a nonreactive saucepan over low heat until warm. Place the raspberries and tarragon in a sterilized, wide-mouthed jar. Pour in the warm vinegar. Seal tight. Let stand in a warm place for two weeks.

Strain the vinegar, pressing the raspberries firmly. Place in a nonreactive saucepan with the honey and bring to a boil. Lower the heat and simmer for 10 minutes. Pour into a sterilized bottle and seal with a new cork. Keep refrigerated.

Yield: 2 cups

RASPBERRY-OAT BRAN MUFFINS

Here's an oat-bran muffin that is lovely to look at, nutritious, and relatively light weight. It's actually a relative to a muffin that was devised for people with diabetes and elevated serum cholesterol.

Preparation tips: This batter needs to stand for approximately 15 minutes before you fill the muffin cups. For an easier clean up, use paper liners sprayed with vegetable oil, such as canola oil.

1 cup oat bran
3/4 cup all-purpose flour
1/2 cup whole-wheat flour
1/3 cup sugar
1 tablespoon baking powder
1/4 teaspoon salt (optional)
1/4 cup canola oil or light butter-margarine blend
2 egg whites
1 cup skim milk
1 teaspoon vanilla extract
1-1/2 cups raspberries, divided
1/2 cup pecans (optional) to sprinkle on top before baking

1. In a large bowl, combine the oat bran, all purpose flour, whole-wheat flour, sugar, baking powder, and salt if desired, stirring the ingredients to mix them well.
2. Cut the butter-margarine blend into bits, and add it to the flour mixture, blending it in with a fork or pastry blender, or two knives.
3. In a small bowl, whisk together the egg whites, milk and vanilla and add them to the dry ingredients, stirring the ingredients until they are just moist.
4. Reserve 12 of the best raspberries, and fold the rest of the berries gently into the batter. Let the batter stand for about 15 minutes.
5. Preheat the oven to 400 degrees F.
6. Distribute the batter among 12 oiled muffin cups. Top each muffin with a reserved berry, and a few pecans.
7. Place the muffin tin in the hot oven, and bake the muffins for 20 to 25 minutes. When the muffins are done, turn them out on their sides onto a rack to cool.

RASPBERRY MUFFINS

This recipe can be a bread type or muffins; it is yummy and versatile. Make it for a special breakfast or brunch. Make days ahead and freeze for later.

1-1/2 cups all-purpose flour (or whole-wheat flour)
1/2 teaspoon baking soda
1/2 teaspoon salt (optional)
1-1/2 teaspoons ground cinnamon
1 cup sugar
1 12-ounce package frozen unsweetened raspberries, thawed
2 eggs, or 4 egg whites, well beaten
2/3 cup vegetable oil
1/2 cup chopped pecans

TOPPING FOR MUFFINS OR BREAD

1/4 cup brown sugar
1 teaspoon orange or lemon zest
1/2 cup pecans

Preheat oven to 400 degrees F.. In medium bowl, mix flour, soda, salt, cinnamon and sugar. Make a well in the center and stir in undrained raspberries and eggs. Thoroughly mix in oil and pecans. Spoon batter into lightly muffin papers lining muffin tins. Muffin cups should be poured full. Batter is heavy and will not overflow. Sprinkle the topping evenly over the tops of muffins or bread. Bake 15-20 minutes. Cool 5 minutes before removing from pan.

If doing a loaf use a 9 x 5 inch pan at 350 degrees F. for 1 hour or until a wooden pick inserted in center comes out clean.

RASPBERRY FLOWER ROLLS

1 package active dry yeast
1/4 cup warm water
1/2 cup milk, scalded
1/4 cup *lite* margarine, or canola oil
2 tablespoons sugar
1/2 teaspoon salt
2-3/4 to 3-1/4 cups sifted all-purpose flour
1 slightly beaten egg or two egg whites

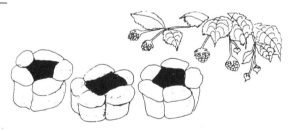

Soften yeast in water. Mix hot milk, oil, sugar, and salt; cool to lukewarm. Add 1 cup flour; beat smooth. Beat in softened yeast and egg. Stir in enough remaining flour to make a soft dough. Turn out on floured surface; knead till smooth and elastic (8 to 10 minutes). Place in lightly oiled bowl, turning once to oil surface. Cover; let rise in warm place till double (about 1 hour). Punch down. Cover; let rest 10 minutes. On lightly floured surface, roll dough to 1/4 inch. Cut with floured 1-1/4 inch biscuit cutter. Oil muffin cups with a vegetable oil spray; arrange 5 circles of dough around sides of each cup and 1 in center. Cover; let almost double (about 30 minutes). Lightly poke down center of each roll and full with raspberry preserves. Bake in hot oven, 400 degrees F., 10 to15 minutes. Brush with melted *lite* margarine.
Yield: about 16 rolls

RASPBERRY DUTCH BABY

This is similar to a popover, but much more dramatic. It is a delight to breakfast, lunch, or a light dinner guests in summer or winter. The eggy batter is best done in a big container, such as a paella pan, or large ceramic, glass and metal baking dishes. Any shape will work but the pan should be fairly shallow—not much over 3 inches deep.

The raspberries are served as a topping or to eat on the side. Round out the menu with a meat such as turkey sausage, ham, or turkey bacon. Have the eggs at room temperature by taking them out of the refrigerator about an hour before you want to start putting the ingredients together.

A tip before you start: have everyone seated at the table before you take the Dutch Baby out of the oven. Whether for family or guests, you don't want them to miss that first spectacular look.

PAN SIZE	"*LITE*" MARGARINE	EGGS	MILK AND FLOUR
2 - 3 qts.	1/4 cup	3	3/4 cup each
3 - 4 qts.	1/3 cup	4	1 cup each
4 - 4 1/2 qts.	1/2 cup	5	1 1/4 cups each
4 1/2 - 5 qts.	1/2 cup	6	1 1/2 cups each

I make this recipe using skim milk and using two egg whites for every egg, a pinch of baking powder, and the results are the same. I have also used half of what is called for in margarine and substituted canola oil, simply sprayed my container with canola oil, and it worked.

Select the recipe proportions to fit your pan, and get out the ingredients you'll need. Put margarine in pan and set into a 425 degree F. oven, then mix batter quickly while margarine melts. Put the "room temperature eggs" in a blender container and whirl at high speed for 1 minute. With motor running, gradually pour in milk, then slowly add flour with a pinch of baking powder; continue whirling for 30 seconds.

Remove the hot pan from oven and pour batter onto the hot melted margarine. Return to oven and bake until puffy and well browned—20 to 25 minutes, depending on the pan. Serve at once.

Use the raspberry syrup, preserves, or any of the sauces. Serve the raspberries with yogurt as a topping or fresh raspberries.

RASPBERRY PANCAKES

Light, nutritious, pancakes with fruit, both within and on top, are a big favorite. This easy way to prepare them will enable you to serve them often.

2/3 cup whole-wheat flour
2/3 cup all-purpose flour
2 tablespoons sugar
1 1/2 teaspoons baking soda
1 egg white
1 egg
2/3 cup plain nonfat or low-fat yogurt
1 cup skim or low-fat milk
1 tablespoon butter or margarine, melted and cooled
2 cups fresh raspberries
1 teaspoon lemon extract

In a large bowl, combine the whole-wheat flour, all-purpose flour, sugar, baking powder, and baking soda. In a medium-sized bowl, lightly beat the egg white and whole egg. Whisk in the yogurt, milk, lemon extract and melted butter or margarine. Stir the liquid mixture into the flour mixture until the two are just combined. Gently fold in the raspberries.

Heat a griddle, preferably one with a non-stick surface (if it is not a non-stick, spray it with vegetable oil before heating it), and pour on a scant 1/4 cup of batter for each pancake. Cook the pancakes over medium-low heat until the bottoms are golden brown. Then flip them over, and cook them on the other side.

SCONES OF RASPBERRY & OATS

1 cup unbleached flour
1/2 cup oat bran
1 cup oats (quick cooking)
2 tablespoons raw sugar
2 teaspoons baking powder
1/2 teaspoon baking soda
2 egg whites
7 ounces lemon or raspberry nonfat yogurt
1/2 cup fresh or frozen raspberries
Skim milk or beaten egg white

1. Using a medium bowl, mix flour, oats, oat bran, sugar, baking powder and soda. Beat the egg whites and stir in to the mixture to make a stiff dough. Gently stir in the raspberries.

2. Form the dough into a ball, and turn onto a floured surface and with flour on your hands, pat the dough into a 7-inch circle.

3. Coat a baking sheet with vegetable spray. Place dough on sheet. Using a knife that has flour on it, cut dough into 12 wedges. Pull the wedge out slightly to leave a 1/2 inch space between them. Brush the tops lightly with skim milk or beaten egg white.

4. Bake at 375 degrees F. for 20 minutes, or until lightly browned. Transfer to a serving plate. Serve with your favorite hot or cold raspberry sauce or fruit spread.   *Yield: 12 scones*

SCANDINAVIAN PANCAKES

These delicate pancakes are delicious and almost fat-free, quite unlike the Swedish pancakes that were so popular when the nation was not so health conscious. Buttermilk is a low-fat ingredient, contrary to its name. You see the liquid is left behind when the cream has been skimmed off the top to make butter.

DRY INGREDIENTS
1 cup whole-wheat flour
1 cup all-purpose flour
1 tablespoon baking soda
$\frac{1}{8}$ teaspoon salt (optional)

WET INGREDIENTS
1 cup egg
3 cups buttermilk
$\frac{1}{4}$ teaspoon vanilla extract

TOPPING
3 cups of raspberries
Low-fat yogurt

1. In a large bowl, combine the dry ingredients, mixing them well.
2. In a medium-sized bowl, beat the eggs lightly, add the buttermilk and vanilla, mixing the ingredients well.
3. Make a well in the dry ingredients, and pour in the wet ingredients, mixing the two just enough to moisten the dry ingredients. When you are ready to cook the pancakes, use a non stick griddle and heat it over medium heat.
4. On the heated griddle, pour sufficient batter to make 4-inch pancakes, four of them at a time on an 11 inch square griddle. Cook the pancakes until they begin to bubble on the surface, then flip them over, and lightly brown them re-oiling the griddle only to prevent the pancakes from sticking to it.
5. Serve the pancakes with the raspberry topping.

FRENCH DESSERT PANCAKES

Sweetened berries and juice
1 cup pancake mix
1 tablespoon sugar
1-$\frac{1}{4}$ cups milk
2 eggs
2 tablespoons canola oil

Prepare and sweeten fresh or frozen berries and set aside. In a bowl, blend last 5 ingredients and beat until almost smooth. Pour 2 tablespoons batter at a time, in lightly oiled, hot skillet. A 6-inch skillet is ideal—tilt it to spread batter. Brown pancakes, adding oil to pan as needed. Keep cakes warm. When done, spread each with sweetened berries, roll and heat in large skillet in berry juice. Top with powdered sugar if desired.

Yield: *Makes about 16 pancakes*

RASPBERRY APPLE TURNOVERS

FILLING

3 tablespoons apple juice
1-1/4 cups finely chopped fresh apples
2 tablespoons sugar

1 tablespoon cornstarch
1/4 cup golden raisins
1/2 cup fresh or frozen raspberries

PASTRY

1-1/4 cups unbleached flour
2 tablespoons sugar
4 tablespoons chilled reduced-fat margarine cut into pieces

1 cup oat bran
1/2 teaspoon baking powder
1/2 cup plus 2 tablespoons nonfat buttermilk

GLAZE

1 tablespoon water
1 tablespoon raw sugar

1 tablespoon beaten egg white

1. For the filling, combine cornstarch and 1 tablespoon of the apple juice, and put aside. Mix the remaining juice, apples, raisins, and sugar in a small saucepan. Cook with cover over medium-low heat for 5-7 minutes, stir constantly, until apples are tender. Add in the raspberries, and cook uncovered for another minute or until the raspberries are soft and begin to break up. Add the cornstarch mixture, and cook, stirring constantly, for another few minutes until mixture is thick. Remove from the heat and put aside to cool.

2. The pastry is made by combining the flour, oat bran, sugar and baking powder, and stir to mix well. Use a pastry cutter to cut in the margarine until the mixture resembles coarse crumbs. Stir in just enough of the buttermilk to make a stiff dough that leaves the sides of the bowl and forms a ball.

3. Work the dough onto a abundantly floured surface, and divide into 2 pieces. Use a rolling pin to roll each piece into an 8 x 12 inch rectangle Use knife to cut each rectangle into six 4-inch squares.

4. In the center of each square, place a rounded tablespoon of filling. Bring one corner over the filling and match up the opposite corner to form a triangle. Seal the turnovers by crimping the edges with the tines of a fork. If fork begins sticking, dip it in sugar.

5. Spray a baking sheet with vegetable oil cooking spray. Lift the turnovers with a spatula and transfer to the baking sheet. Combine egg white and water, and brush over the tops of the pastries. Sprinkle 1/4 teaspoon of raw sugar over each turnover. Preheat oven 375 degree F. and bake for 20 minutes.

*H*aving grown up on homemade raspberry jam, I just cannot imagine any mornings without it. But for me, it is equally difficult to actually plan whipping up a batch. It is only after the tempestuous little critters threaten to rot, and I have eaten all that I can of them fresh, do I consider sugaring and warming them. This, of course does happen on a regular basis in the months of July and August.

The secret for brilliantly colored and fresh-tasting raspberry jam is to cook it in small batches for the shortest possible time. A wide pan is needed, perhaps a 12 inch stainless-steel or other noncorrosive skillet or saute pan large enough to accommodate 4 cups of raspberries. For making greater quantities of jam, simply repeat the procedure until all the raspberries are used up.

RASPBERRY JAM

4 cups fresh raspberries, picked over, rinsed and drained if necessary
3 cups sugar
$\frac{1}{4}$ cup strained fresh lemon juice

1. Place raspberries, sugar and lemon juice in 12-inch stainless-steel or noncorrosive skillet or saute pan; stir to combine. Let stand, uncovered, at room temperature for 1 hour, stirring occasionally until sugar is dissolved.
2. Heat raspberries and their juices over medium-high heat to a rolling boil, stirring often. Boil raspberry mixture until candy thermometer registers 220°*, or 3 minutes for a soft jam, 4 minutes for a stiffer jam. Skim foam from surface.
3. Ladle jam into sterilized half-pint jars and seal with canning lids, following manufacturer's instructions. Cool on wire rack; store in cool dark place. Or if jam is to be used within a few weeks, store in tightly covered containers, in refrigerator.

*TIP: Boil mixture until it passes the jelly test, as follows. Let a small amount of the mixture fall from the edge of a metal spoon; when the last few drops coalesce and drop from spoon in a sheet, the jam is ready.

MICRO TIP: Place 4 cups of rinsed drained raspberries in deep 3-quart glass casserole. Pour sugar and lemon juice over berries; toss. Let stand, uncovered, at room temperature 1 hour. Microwave on high power until boiling rapidly, about 9 minutes, stirring once. Stir well; microwave 9 minutes longer. Remove casserole to wire rack and cool to room temperature or ladle while hot into sterilized jars. Seal and store.

Tip: For a jalepeño variety, add 1 tsp. jalepeño juice to $\frac{1}{2}$ pint of jam.
Yield: 2-$\frac{1}{2}$ cups

PEACH RASPBERRY JAM

10 cups well ripened peaches
3 (three ounce) packages raspberry jello
10 cups sugar

Crush peaches in large heavy kettle, add sugar and bring to rolling boil. Turn heat to medium and boil for 20 minutes, stirring often. Add 3 packages of jello and stir until completely dissolved. Turn off heat. Pour fruit into jars. Seal with melted paraffin.

PEACH RASPBERRY JAM USING GELATIN

10 cups mashed peaches
12 cups sugar
2 packages frozen or 2 pints fresh raspberries
2 packages gelatin (family size) raspberry flavor

Chop peaches in blender. Mix sugar, peaches and berries. Boil 30 minutes. Add gelatin and boil 5 minutes more. Pour in jars and seal.

WILD RASPBERRY JAM

Use ³/₄ cup sugar per cup of berries. Crush berries, add sugar, cook down on medium heat until slightly thickened (about ¹/₂ hour). Put in sterilized jars and seal with paraffin.

PEAR-RASPBERRY JAM

2 pounds fully ripe pears
¹/₄ cup lemon juice
1 package (10-ounce) frozen raspberries, thawed
6 cups sugar
3 ounces liquid pectin
Paraffin

Preparation time: 45 Minutes   Cooking time: 10 Minutes

1. Peel, core, and grind pears. Put raspberries in 1-quart measure and add ground pears to equal 4 cups. Place large pan and add lemon juice.
2. Mix in sugar, bring to roll boil, and boil hard 1 minute, stirring constantly. Remove from heat and stir in pectin. Skim foam and stir occasionally for 5 minutes.
3. Stir and skim foam alternately for 5 minutes. Add extract and stir. Ladle into sterilized glasses. Seal with ¹/₈ inch layer hot paraffin or use air-tight lids.

Yields: 10 medium glasses

CHERRY-RASPBERRY FREEZER JAM

1-$^1/_2$ pints raspberries or blackberries
5-$^1/_4$ cups sugar
$^3/_4$ cup water
1-$^1/_2$ pounds fully ripe sour cherries
1 box (1-$^3/_4$ ounce) powdered pectin

Preparation time: 40 Minutes   Cooking time: 5 Minutes

1. Crush raspberries. Pit and grind cherries. Measure 1-$^1/_2$ cups each into bowl. Stir in sugar and set aside.

2. Mix water and pectin in saucepan. Boil 1 minute, stirring constantly. Stir into fruits and continue stirring 3 minutes.

3. Ladle into jars. Cover at once with tight lids. When jam is set, store in freezer.

Yields: 7 medium jars

THE BASIC SAUCE (SCANDINAVIAN)

A lovely finishing touch for poultry or pork.

10 ounces fresh or frozen raspberries
2 tablespoons dry white wine
1 tablespoon orange liqueur (Cointreau, 70 proof, french, is my favorite; Grand Marnier,
80 proof, french, triple orange; and Salicsa, 63 proof, a Costa Rican
product. Kirsch is another good liqueur with raspberries.)
2 tablespoons cornstarch
1 tablespoon butter

Place fresh or thawed raspberries in blender container and blend until smooth. In a medium saucepan, combine wine, orange liqueur and cornstarch. Stir in raspberries and butter. Cook, stirring constantly, until mixture is thickened and bubbly. Cook and stir for 2 minutes more. Strain through a sieve and serve. If you are using fresh raspberries reserve $1/2$ cup. Garnish the sieved sauce with fresh raspberries by gently turning them into the finished product.

THE EASY SAUCE

A quick, American and low-fat version of the above recipe.

I use this often when I have unexpected guests. It is a perfect dessert when used as a topping on low fat frozen yogurt. For a lovely, fancier version use parfait glasses. Spoon layers of frozen yogurt, oreo chocolate cookies crumbs, bits of pecans or walnuts with the raspberry sauce layers. As the final topping, use fresh raspberries and nuts.

10 ounces fresh or frozen raspberries
1 tablespoon orange liqueur, Kirsch, or an apricot liqueur or brandy

In a medium saucepan, combine liqueur and raspberries. Add 1 tablespoon of sugar if this sauce is for a dessert. Cook about one minute until sugar is dissolved. Strain if you have a problem eating the seeds and do not want 65% of the valuable roughage. Serve hot or cold.

RASPBERRY GLAZE

Fruit juice is the base of this quick thick sauce or glaze that goes well with fresh fruit, frozen yogurt, topping for cheesecake, or on a slice of pound cake.

2 cups cranberry-raspberry juice
2 tablespoons Kirsch or orange liqueur
2 tablespoons of cornstarch or 1 teaspoon cornstarch for a thinner sauce
1 cup frozen unsweetened raspberries (not thawed)

In a large saucepan or skillet, bring juice to a boil over high heat. Cook until reduced to about $1/2$ cup, about 10 minutes. In a small bowl, stir together Kirsch or orange liqueur and cornstarch; whisk into the sauce and cook until it has thickened and become clear again. Remove the pan from the heat and stir in raspberries; let stand briefly until the berries have thawed. Stir again. Serve warm or cool.

Yield: Makes 1 cup

HOT BERRY JUBILEE SAUCE

10 ounces raspberry or blackberry preserves
2 cups frozen unsweetened raspberries
1 tablespoon cornstarch
1/2 cup raspberry flavored brandy

Cook preserves and raspberries together over medium heat for 3 minutes. Dissolve cornstarch into heated mixture. Once cornstarch is dissolved, add brandy. Cook and stir until clear and thickened. Serve hot over frozen yogurt or ice cream or spoon over slices of cheese cake.

QUICK THREE BERRY-CHERRY SAUCE

One 16 ounce can of Cherry pie filling, any brand
10 ounces fresh or frozen raspberries
10 ounces fresh or frozen blueberries
10 ounces fresh or frozen blackberries

Divide these berries and cherry pie mixture into 4 zip-lock freezer bags. Use berry bags in appropriate amounts to top for cheese cakes, pound cake, short cake, frozen yogurt or ice cream, or combine two packages and fill a pie shell.

RASPBERRY SAUCE FOR FRUIT

Nectarines, peaches, apricots, kiwis, oranges, cantaloupe, and large strawberries (I'm sure there are others), are made better by this yummie sauce. The sauce can be prepared ahead, then assembled with the fruit just before serving time.

2 teaspoons sugar
1/2 cup dry white wine
6 ripe oranges, nectarines or peaches etc. peeled, pitted, and sliced or put into smaller appealing pieces *(about 5 cups of fruit)*
1 10-ounce package unsweetened frozen raspberries, thawed and liquid reserved
Fresh mint for garnish (optional)

1. In a large glass or enameled saucepan or one with non-stick surface, combine the sugar and wine, and bring the ingredients to a boil. Reduce the heat, and add the nectarines. Cover the saucepan tightly, and simmer the fruit for 2 minutes. Using a slotted spoon, transfer the fruit to a platter to cool.

2. Continue cooking the poached liquid in the uncovered saucepan over high heat until the liquid becomes syrupy. Set the liquid aside to cool.

3. To prepare the sauce, pour off all but 2 tablespoons of berry liquid to a blender, and puree the mixture until it is smooth. Strain the puree through a fine sieve, pressing on the solids to extract all their juice. Discard the seeds.

4. Spoon the sauce onto individual plates. Divide the fruit wedges or pieces among the plates, arranging them like the spokes of a wheel, if possible. Then spoon the reserved poaching liquid over the fruit. Serve the dessert at room temperature, garnish with the mint (if desired).

RASPBERRY "RELISHED"

2 cups raspberries
1 cup cranberries
1 cup water
1-1/2 cups sugar

Bring cranberries to a boil in the water. Add sugar and stir until completely dissolved. Add raspberries and simmer for 3 minutes.
Serve with pork, poultry, or fish.

RASPBERRY-CRANBERRY CHUTNEY

This chutney can be made quickly and is more interesting than cranberry sauce. It is the perfect alternative sauce to serve with turkey and pork dishes.

1 cup frozen unsweetened raspberries (not thawed)
1 cup fresh or frozen cranberries
2/3 cup orange marmalade
1/3 cup chopped shallots (2 large)
2 tablespoons balsamic vinegar
1 teaspoon ground ginger
1/2 teaspoon ground allspice

In a saucepan, combine raspberries, cranberries, marmalade, shallots, vinegar, ginger and allspice; bring up heat and then simmer. Cook over low heat, stirring occasionally, until the mixture has thickened, about 7 minutes. Serve warm or cold. Makes 1-1/2 cups.

RASPBERRY SALSA

1 cup fresh raspberries
2 tablespoons chopped fresh mint
2 tablespoons chopped fresh basil
2 teaspoons seeded and finely chopped jalapeño (or to taste for wimps and undeveloped palates)
2 teaspoons fresh lemon juice
1/4 teaspoon kosher salt
Freshly ground pepper to taste

Coarsely chop half of the raspberries and toss them with the whole berries, mint, basil and jalapeño. Toss with the lemon juice, salt and pepper. Let stand no longer then 10 minutes before serving. Use on grilled chicken, salmon, venison or pork.

RASPBERRY APPLESAUCE

Simplicity itself, applesauce from a jar becomes quite special when warmed and laced with raspberries.

1 cup prepared "chunky" applesauce
2/3 cup frozen unsweetened raspberries (not thawed)

In a small "microwaveable" bowl, stir together applesauce and raspberries. Cover with plastic wrap and microwave on high power (100%) for 1-1/2 minutes, or until heated through. Stir gently to avoid breaking down the raspberries.

(Alternatively, warm applesauce in a small saucepan over medium heat. Remove from the heat and stir in raspberries; let stand until they are thawed.)

Yield: Makes 1-1/2 cups

RASPBERRY HONEY (A GREAT SYRUP)

This is so easy you just won't believe it. It is so good as a variation of honey but is a bit thinner, so much so that it makes a perfect syrup too.

3 cups "local" honey or clover honey
3 cups fresh raspberries picked over

In a 2 quart pan, bring the honey to a boil and add the raspberries and stir with a spoon. Cool. Pour into pint containers and cover with a lid. I have stored this honey in the refrigerator for a year! If you are storing in a cool place, you need to seal the air tight lids with paraffin. Do this by melting paraffin in a metal container. Let this melted paraffin cool slightly but remain a liquid. Then put the bottle lid in and out, of the paraffin quickly. I do the quick-dip in the paraffin twice for a good seal. These jars of honey make great gifts from your kitchen.

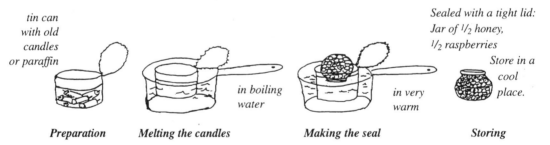

FRAMBOISE SAUCE

1 10-ounce package frozen raspberries, defrosted
1/4 cup sugar
2 tablespoons framboise (raspberry liqueur)

Puree and strain berries. Combine with sugar and framboise.

MELBA SAUCE

This glowing, ruby-red sauce needn't be reserved for the classic "Melba" desserts of just vanilla ice cream laid down on poached peaches or other kinds of fruit. It is the perfect company for almost any ice cream. The darkest chocolate ice cream, tapioca pudding and other puddings, cakes and yogurts are made better with this distinguished sauce.

Currant jelly adds the body which permits the shorter cooking time and preserves the unique raspberry flavor. The jelly also makes using cornstarch unnecessary. Do enhance this sauce by adding a nip of framboise or Creme de Cassis, peach or cherry brandy or the orange liqueurs, just before serving.

6 cups fresh raspberries, picked over, rinsed and drained if necessary
1 cup sugar
1 cup currant jelly, preferable made without added pectin
3 tablespoons strained fresh lemon juice

1. If you prefer a sauce without seeds: Puree raspberries in blender or food processor, place in fine-mesh sieve set over bowl. Press puree through sieve with back of large spoon to remove seeds; discards seeds.
2. Stir raspberry puree, sugar, currant jelly and lemon juice in large sauce pan until completely blended. Heat over high heat to boiling, stirring constantly. Boil, stirring constantly, 2 minutes; skim any foam from surface.
3. Ladle hot sauce into half-pint canning jars, leaving 1/4-inch headspace.

Adjust lids according to manufacturer's directions; process jars in boiling water bath for 5 minutes. Cool jars on wire rack; store in cool dark place. Or if sauce is to be used within a few weeks, omit processing and store, tightly covered, in the refrigerator.

Yield: About 4 cups

RASPBERRY BUTTER

Equal amounts raspberries and unsalted butter
Half as much Confectioners sugar

Mix raspberries and butter together. Add confectioners sugar. Use on scones, thin cookies or croissants.

CREAM DE CREAM

This is the cream that the French use in their delicious raspberry tarts. It is wonderful for dessert at lunch, dinner or for breakfast.

2 eggs
1/2 cup sugar
1 tablespoon all-purpose flour
Juice of 1 lemon, freshly squeezed
1 cup pineapple juice
1 pint whipping cream, whipped
2 pints fresh raspberries

Mix the eggs, sugar, flour, lemon juice, and pineapple juice in a heavy saucepan. Bring to a boil, and simmer until thickened, stirring constantly. Cool thoroughly, and fold in whipped cream. Pour cream in pastry dough tart shells and arrange berries on top of the cream. Glaze with either the raspberry glaze or apricot glaze. Keep in the refrigerator until ready to serve.

Another choice with this cream is to arrange the berries in individual dessert dishes and pour the cream over the top of berries. Garnish with mint leaves and a berrie or two.

RASPBERRY SYRUP

What a treat for pancakes, popovers and aebelskiver.

2 quarts ripe raspberries
3-1/2 cups water
4-1/2 cups sugar or 3-1/2 cups sugar for a thinner syrup

Crush berries and combine with water in a heavy kettle. Bring to a boil and boil rapidly for 10 minutes. Lower heat and simmer for 5 more minutes. Strain juice through jelly bag and measure. You should have about 5 cups of juice. Add sugar to juice and boil rapidly for 12 minutes until syrup begins to thicken. Do not overcook, or it will gel.

Pour into sterilized bottles and cork. Dip the cork and approximately one inch of the bottle neck, into a melted paraffin mixture to insure proper sealing.

ELEGANT PAN-SEARED DUCK BREASTS WITH RASPBERRY SAUCE

1 tablespoon olive oil
2 small boneless, skinless duck breasts, or two Cornish hens, or one turkey breast
1 teaspoon salt
Freshly ground pepper to taste
1/4 cup raspberry vinegar
1 cup fresh raspberries
1 large orange, sections cut from membranes
2 tablespoons heavy cream *or for a low fat alternative:*
  2 tablespoons of low fat yogurt that has been put in a sieve overnight to drain off liquid

1. Heat the oil in a large, heavy skillet over medium-high heat. Add the duck breasts (or your choice of poultry) and sear for 5 minutes. Lower the heat to medium and cook for 3 minutes longer. Turn the duck over and cook for 3 minutes. Cover the pan and cook until the duck is tender and still pink in the center, about 4 minutes longer. Remove the duck from the pan. Season with 1 teaspoon of salt and pepper to taste and keep warm.

2. Add the vinegar to the skillet and cook, scraping the bottom of the pan with a wooden spoon. Add 2/3 cup of the raspberries and the orange sections and cook for 3 minutes. Stir in the cream, or yogurt, remaining salt and pepper to taste. Cook for 1 minute.

3. Cut the duck into thin slices and fan them out onto four plates. Spoon the sauce over the duck, garnish with the remaining raspberries and serve immediately.

Yield: *4 servings*

RASPBERRY VINEGAR, BASIL & TOMATOES

1 cup raspberry vinegar
2 tablespoon olive oil
3 - 4 or more cloves garlic, minced
1 teaspoon black pepper
1 teaspoon salt (optional)
1 cup freshly chopped basil
4 tomatoes

Whisk together vinegar, oil, garlic, pepper, salt, and basil. Slice tomatoes and marinate in dressing for at least 3 - 4 hours. Cover and refrigerate.

SALMON WITH PINK RASPBERRY SAUCE

2 tablespoons *lite* margarine
2 6-ounce fresh salmon steaks[*]
2 teaspoon fresh lemon juice
Sea salt and pepper

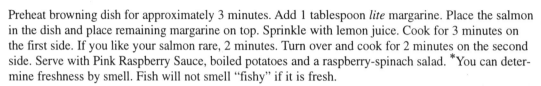

Preheat browning dish for approximately 3 minutes. Add 1 tablespoon *lite* margarine. Place the salmon in the dish and place remaining margarine on top. Sprinkle with lemon juice. Cook for 3 minutes on the first side. If you like your salmon rare, 2 minutes. Turn over and cook for 2 minutes on the second side. Serve with Pink Raspberry Sauce, boiled potatoes and a raspberry-spinach salad. [*]You can determine freshness by smell. Fish will not smell "fishy" if it is fresh.

PINK RASPBERRY SAUCE

This sauce is fairly wonderful and after you have had it on salmon you may want it on other kinds of fish. It goes well on all your favorite broiled fish, as well as on the salmon recipe above.

1-$^1/_2$ tablespoons *lite* margarine
2 tablespoons flour
$^1/_2$ cup boiling, salted water
1 egg yolk, optional
1 tablespoon cold water
6 tablespoons *lite* margarine
Juice of $^1/_2$ lemon
$^1/_2$ cup raspberries, fresh or unthawed, unsweetened, frozen berries

Melt 1-$^1/_2$ tablespoons margarine in a skillet. Stir in flour until well blended. Add boiling water and whisk until thickened. Beat the egg yolk with the cold water. Remove skillet from heat and stir in the egg yolk. Add 6 tablespoons margarine and stir until melted. Add the raspberries. Strain the sauce, if you do not want the seeds and roughage, and add the lemon juice.

Yield: 2 servings

CARROTS & PARSNIPS WITH RASPBERRIES

6 carrots, peeled and diced into small pieces
3 parsnips, peeled and diced into small pieces
4 $^1/_2$ tablespoons water
$^1/_2$ teaspoon salt
$^1/_2$ cup raspberries
3 tablespoons yogurt
3 teaspoons honey
3 teaspoons raspberry vinegar
1$^1/_2$ tablespoons rosemary

Combine carrots, parsnips, water and salt. Simmer until tender. Add raspberries, yogurt, honey and raspberry vinegar and toss gently. Cook over mild heat for an additional 2 - 4 minutes. Sprinkle with rosemary.

TROUT-ALMOND WITH RASPBERRY SAUCE

2 large, fresh trout
$1/2$ cup slivered almonds
$1/2$ cup fresh bread crumbs
$1/2$ cup *lite* butter or *lite* margarine

Buy the trout filleted or fillet yourself. Coat the fish with the mixture of almonds and bread crumbs. Saute in butter until done, and top with raspberry sauce.

RASPBERRY FISH SAUCE
1-$1/2$ ounces red vine vinegar
1-$1/2$ ounces white wine
$1/4$ cup minced shallots
$1/8$ teaspoon white pepper
$1/2$ cup *lite* butter or *lite* margarine, chilled
$1/2$ cup fresh raspberries

In a small skillet combine vinegar, wine, shallots, and pepper. Reduce by cooking to 2 tablespoons. Slowly, whisking constantly, add butter or margarine. Add raspberries, mash by whisking them about. Strain if seeds are a problem, and serve the warm sauce over warm trout.

"RASPBURIED" CHICKEN

Accompany this glamorous dish with wild rice, great green vegetables and raspberry yams. Bring the raspberries back in the dessert. Bake this recipe in a Robertopf™ terra cotta clay baker, if you own one. Immersed in water before each use, the unglazed clay container absorbs the water, which is then released during cooking, blending with the the natural juices of whatever is inside. If you do not own a Robertopf™, use a covered baking dish, adding $1/2$ cup of chicken stock to the covered dish.

3 to 4 -pound chicken, whole
10 small yellow onions, whole or quartered
4 tablespoons raspberry vinegar
2 cups chopped fresh tomatoes with juices
6 small, peeled potatoes

Place chicken in the baking dish. Stuff 4-5 onions inside chicken and place the remaining around the sides. Pour raspberry vinegar or raspberry-tarragon vinegar over chicken. Layer chopped tomatoes over chicken top. Along the sides put peeled small potatoes. Cover Robertopf™ pot and place in center of cold oven. Set oven to 400 degrees F. and bake for 1-$1/2$ to 2 hours. If using another type of roasting pan, set oven temperature at 375 degrees F..

Yield: 4 portions

COLORADO AXIS BUFFALO/VENISON WITH RASPBERRY PEPPER SAUCE

This is a sauce that you can be very proud to serve. This main course goes quite nicely with seasonal fresh vegetables and potatoes or rice.

4 5-ounce buffalo or venison loins

Clean and de-fat loins. Cook the meat to the state of doneness that you and your guests desire and serve the sauce in a pouring pitcher, so that each person can add the amount they want, and it is wonderfully delicious! You could probably serve this sauce on cardboard and the cardboard would be gobbled down!

RASPBERRY PEPPER SAUCE:

1 tablespoon olive oil
1 rib celery diced
1/2 onion diced
1/2 carrot diced
1/2 can tomato paste
2 serrano chilies (can use mild mexican style green chilies)
1 tablespoon chopped fresh herbs, sage, rosemary, and thyme (substitute 1 teaspoon if using dried herbs)
1 cup good quality red wine (we used Morgon, Red Beaujolais, 1994)
3 cups of veal stock (or Better Than Bullion Beef Base, as it is non-fat)
2 pints fresh raspberries pureed *or as you add the raspberries mash them against the pan instead of doing the puree*
8 whole berries for garnish
2 tablespoons picked green peppercorns
Salt and pepper to taste

Saute vegetables in hot oil until light brown in color. Stir in tomato paste and continue cooking until caramelized. Add wine, mix, cook until syrupy. Add the stock with the raspberries and cook until you have reduced the liquid to 1-1/2 cups.

A quicker version is to cook the sauce as you are getting the vegetables cooked and the table set. If it has not reduced to half the volume, not to worry. It will still be divine. This can be made a day in advance or made and then frozen.

RASPBERRY HONEY YAMS

4 medium yams
3/4 cup raspberry honey
1 orange, peeled and sectioned or 1 6-ounce can mandarin oranges
3/4 cup chopped walnuts or 1 cup sunflower seeds
1/2 cup nonfat margarine or butter

Peel and boil yams until tender. Put yams, honey, oranges and margarine in a medium bowl and mash until well mixed. Put mixture into a 9 x 12 inch oiled glass baking dish. Sprinkle chopped nuts on top and bake at 350 degrees F. for 30 minutes.

CHOCOLATE HAZELNUT, RICOTTA MOUSSE, RASPBERRY-ORANGE LAYER CAKE

This cake is a beautiful work of art. It should be prepared for a very special occasion. In making this cake, you will be creating a delicious dessert and in following the pastry chef's directions you will be learning valuable lessons in the culinary arts. Begin this cake knowing it is a learning experience.

10 ounces peeled hazelnuts or pecans
1/2 cup cornstarch
7 ounces semi-sweet chocolate
1/4 cup orange-flavored liqueur
1 teaspoon vanilla
5 eggs, separated
1/3 cup and 1/4 cup sugar
1/4 teaspoon cream of tartar
Orange Syrup
Ricotta Mousse Raspberry Sauce
1/2 cup raspberries
Chocolate leaves, optional

1. Preheat oven to 350 degrees F.

2. Line bottom of pullman pan with parchment paper. Butter and flour sides of 17 x11 inch jelly roll pan. (It is important to use the designated pan for this recipe. They are available through restaurant-supply stores and some gourmet shops).

3. Finely grind enough hazelnuts to yield 1/2 cup plus 2 tablespoons by placing nuts in blender or food processor fitted with metal blade. Using 1-second pulses, grind to fine powder. Grind small amounts of nuts at one time, being careful not to grind too long and liquefy them. Mix nuts with cornstarch and set aside.

4. Chop chocolate into small pieces and place in top of double boiler. Add liqueur and vanilla. Place over simmering water until chocolate is just melted. Remove from heat and stir gently to combine ingredients. Set aside and allow to cool to room temperature.

5. Beat egg yolks with 1/3 cup sugar in large bowl until slightly thick. Slowly beat in melted chocolate. In medium bowl, beat egg whites until foamy. Add cream of tartar and continue beating until soft peaks form. Gradually add 1/4 cup sugar and beat until whites are stiff but still glossy. Fold 1/4 of whites into chocolate mixture. Gently fold in remaining whites

6. Spread batter evenly on prepared pan. Bake 10 to 12 minutes or until cake begins to pull away from sides of pan. Cool in pan 10 minutes. Run knife around edges of cake to loosen from sides of pan. Place a sheet of waxed paper or parchment paper over cake. Place a large wire cooling rack or baking sheet over cake and carefully invert cake onto rack. Cover with clean dish towel and cool completely. When cake is cool, carefully slide onto flat surface. Peel off parchment paper and cut cake into four 11 1/2 x 4-inch rectangles. Cover cake layers with plastic wrap and set aside until ready to assemble.

7. To assemble cake, line bottom and sides of 12 x 4 inch straight-sided loaf pan with parchment paper. Tape top edges of paper to pan to keep paper in position. When Ricotta Mousse begins to thicken, but is still pourable, pour 1/4 into bottom of pan; smooth into even layer with rubber spatula. Carefully position one cake layer on top of mousse. Cake breaks easily, so use a long wide, offset spatula or cardboard rectangle to lift layers into place when assembling. Brush cake with small amount of Orange Syrup.

8. Continue to fill cake pan with alternating layers of mousse and cake, ending with layer of cake, and brushing each layer with Orange Syrup. Cover tightly with plastic wrap and chill until firmly set, about 4 hours.

9. To unmold, run knife between pan and parchment paper. Invert pan onto serving platter. Tap on pan to loosen cake, then gently lift pan away from cake. If pan does not slide off easily, wrap a hot, wet towel around outside of pan for a few minutes. Remove parchment paper from sides and tip of cake. Trim slice from each end of cake to reveal alternating layers of cake and mousse. Brush cake sides with small amount of Orange Syrup before pressing 1 cup chopped hazelnuts onto sides. Decorate top with alternating rows of raspberries and finely chopped hazelnuts. To serve, spoon a small amount of Raspberry Sauce onto plate alongside of cake slice. Decorate each slice with raspberry and chocolate or mint leaves.

ORANGE SYRUP

1/3 cup freshly squeezed orange juice
2 tablespoons sugar
2 tablespoons orange-flavored liqueur

In a small saucepan, combine orange juice and sugar. Bring to boil, stirring until sugar is dissolved. Remove from heat, cool to room temperature and add orange liqueur.

RICOTTA MOUSSE

2-1/2 cups Ricotta cheese
2 tablespoons orange-flavored liqueur
2 teaspoons vanilla
1-3/4 cups whipping cream
2 tablespoons unflavored gelatin
7 tablespoons freshly squeezed orange juice
3 eggs
3 egg yolks
1/2 cup sugar

1. Combine ricotta, orange liqueur and vanilla in food processor fitted with steel blade; process until smooth. Spoon mixture into large bowl and set aside. Beat whipping cream until soft peaks form, then refrigerate. Sprinkle gelatin over orange juice in small bowl and set aside to soften.

2. Combine eggs, yolks and sugar in large bowl. Beat with mixer or balloon whisk until well blended. Place mixture in top of double boiler over boiling water and continue beating until mixture triples in volume and holds soft peaks, about 5 to 10 minutes. Just before eggs reach soft peak stage, place gelatin mixture over small pot of simmering water and stir until gelatin is just dissolved. Remove egg mixture from heat and add gelatin, continuing to beat until mixture cools to room temperature—about 5 minutes. Stir 1/4 of of mixture into Ricotta; then fold in remaining egg mixture. Fold in softly whipped cream. Place mousse over bowl of ice water and gently stir with folding motion until mixture just begins to thicken. Remove from ice and immediately assemble cake.

RASPBERRY SAUCE

3 baskets fresh raspberries, about 3 cups
1/4 cup sugar
1 teaspoon lemon juice
2 tablespoons orange-flavored liqueur

In food processor, puree raspberries. Strain to remove seeds. Stir in sugar and lemon juice. Refrigerate. When ready to serve cake, stir in liqueur.

RASPBERRY NUT DESSERT TORTE

CRUST:
2 cups finely chopped walnuts
2 tablespoons canola oil
2 tablespoons sugar

FILLING:
1 cup sugar
$3/4$ cup unbleached cake flour
1 teaspoon baking powder
$1/2$ cup canola oil
2 large eggs or 4 egg whites
$1-1/2$ teaspoons almond extract
8 ounces frozen whole raspberries, drained
$1/2$ cup coarsely chopped walnuts
Confectioners sugar

Preheat oven to 350 degrees F.

CRUST:

Combine in food processor or mix by hand and press over bottom and halfway up sides of a 10-inch spring form pan.

FILLING:

In a bowl, combine flour, baking powder and sugar and set aside. Using the whisk attachment of a mixer or by hand, combine oil, eggs and almond extract. Mix in the flour-sugar mixture. With a spatula, fold in raspberries and walnuts. Pour into greased spring form pan. Bake in preheated oven for 45 minutes or until the cake is set. Release from pan. Sprinkle with confectioners sugar. Decorate with fresh raspberries.

CHOCOLATE RASPBERRY ROLL

1 container (12 ounces) raspberry yogurt
$1/2$ cup raspberries preserves
1 package (9 ounces) chocolate wafer cookies (40)
$1/2$ pint fresh raspberries

In a small bowl, mix yogurt and raspberry preserves. Use half of this mixture for the filling between the wafers and the other half to frost the entire roll. Spread 1 teaspoon of the mixture on one side of each of 7 wafers. Use a plain wafer on top of the stack. Repeat and make 5 stacks. Turn stacks on their side on a platter. Frost with remaining mixture. Freeze 3 - 4 hours or overnight, covering well. To serve, cut in slices and top with fresh raspberries.

Layer 4 stacks

Frost

Slice

1881 RASPBERRY ROLL

This is a very old recipe and I would like for you to see from the way it is written, how different we approach cooking today. The ingredients and the way they are measured tell us it is 1881. To make this non-fat recipe, substitute the butter and lard for Prune Butter, page 15. You can substitute nonfat yogurt for the cream. For the brandy, use a peach or apricot.

Roll

Quart flour
1 tablespoon butter
1 tablespoon lard
1 teaspoon fine salt
Teacup water
1-1/2 pound raspberries

Sauce

2 tablespoons butter
1-1/2 teacups powdered sugar
1/2 teaspoon grated nutmeg
1 wine glass brandy

Add butter and lard to flour. Work lard and butter into flour until mixed. Add salt and a teacup of water, a little at a time, until dough is thick enough to roll on pastry block. Sprinkle flour on the surface to keep dough from sticking. Roll 3 pieces of dough as thin as pie crust, about 18 x 10 inch in size. Lay 1 sheet down and cover with raspberries, then lay out second and third layers, covering all with raspberries. Sprinkle dry sugar over each layer of raspberries before rolling in cloth.

Roll all 3 layers together as you would a towel, then wet a white cloth in cold water and wrap it around the roll, sewing it tightly, then put the roll into a pot of boiling water. Put enough water to cover the roll. Do not cook over 20 minutes.

Beat the butter and sugar together until it is a light cream. Add the nutmeg and brandy into the cream and beat well.

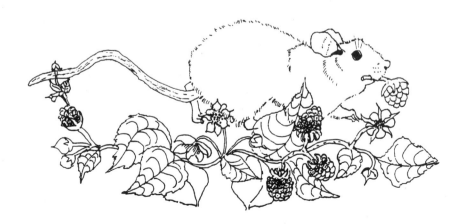

RASPBERRY COFFEECAKE

CAKE:

3/4 cup milk
2 packages active dry yeast
6 tablespoons unsalted butter, at room temperature, and some for oiling the bowl and pan
2 teaspoons grated orange zest
6 tablespoons sugar
3 eggs, beaten
3/4 cup orange juice
4 cups all-purpose flour, and some for kneading
2 teaspoons kosher salt
1 cup fresh raspberries

FILLING:

2/3 cup all-purpose flour
1/2 cup brown sugar
1/2 cup sliced almonds
1-1/2 teaspoon yeast, with a pinch of salt
3 tablespoons unsalted butter, cold and cut into pieces
1 cup fresh raspberries
1 cup confectioners sugar
2 tablespoons fresh lemon juice

1. Preheat oven to 375 degrees F.

2. To make the cake, heat the milk to lukewarm. Place in a large bowl and whisk in the yeast. Let stand for 5 minutes. Cream together the butter, orange zest and sugar. Stir in the eggs one at a time. Slowly stir in the orange juice. Whisk the butter mixture into the yeast mixture. Stir in 1 cup of the flour. Stir in another cup of the flour, the salt and the raspberries. Gradually work in the remaining flour.

3. On a well-floured surface, knead the dough. Place the dough into a large buttered bowl, cover with a towel and set aside in a warm place until doubled in bulk, about 1 hour.

4. Meanwhile, to make the filling, place the flour, brown sugar, almonds and salt in a food processor and pulse until combined. Add the butter and pulse until well mixed. Set aside.

5. Punch down the dough and roll it out into a 15 x 17 inch rectangle. Spread the filling over the dough and press it in with the rolling pin. Scatter the raspberries evenly over the dough like a jelly roll.

6. Butter a large bundt or kugelhopf pan. Place the dough in the pan and pinch the ends together to seal securely. Cover and let rise until doubled, about 1 hour.

7. Bake for 20 minutes. Lower the heat to 350 degrees and bake until browned and cooked through, about 50 minutes longer. Let stand for 10 minutes. Combine the confectioners sugar and lemon juice. Turn the cake out of the pan and drizzle with the glaze.

Yield: *About 20 servings*

HONEY LEMON UN-CHEESECAKE WITH RASPBERRY SAUCE

1- 10 1/2 ounces package tofu, drained
1-1/4 cup no-fat cottage cheese
1/2 cup honey
3 tablespoons oil
3 tablespoons + 1 teaspoon lemon juice
1 1/4 teaspoons vanilla
1 tablespoon + 1 teaspoon grated lemon zest
1- 8 inch graham cracker type crust

Preheat oven to 350 degrees F. Process tofu, honey and oil in blender or food processor. Add next 3 ingredients and blend another 30 seconds. Pour filling into crust and bake for 1 hour. Chill. Serve topped with raspberry sauce.

RASPBERRY SAUCE:

2 cups raspberries
2 tablespoons sugar

Puree berries, strain and discard seeds. Combine puree with sugar in small pan and simmer 5 minutes Cool.

Yield: Serves 8-9

RASPBERRY UPSIDE-DOWN CAKE

2 tablespoons frozen lemon or orange concentrate, thawed
1/4 cup raw sugar
1-1/4 cups fresh or frozen raspberries
1-1/4 cups unbleached flour
1/3 cup oat flour
1-1/2 teaspoons baking powder
1/2 cup sugar
2/3 cup skim milk
1/3 cup honey
2 egg whites
1 teaspoon vanilla

1. Preheat the oven to 350 degree F.
2. Spray the bottom of an 8 inch square pan with vegetable oil. Spread the juice concentrate on the bottom of the pan, and sprinkle with raw sugar. Arrange the raspberries over the raw sugar.
3. Combine the flours, baking powder, and sugar, and stir to mix well. Add other ingredients and stir well.
4. Spreading evenly, pour the batter over the raspberries, and place dish in the middle of the oven. Bake for 35-45 minutes or until the wooden pick, placed in the center of pan, comes out clean indicating doneness.
5. Cool for 10-15 minutes before serving. Vanilla nonfat frozen yogurt makes a great topping for this dessert.

Yield: 9-10 servings

CHOCOLATE TRUFFLE CHEESECAKE WITH RASPBERRY CREME SAUCE

CRUST

1-$^1/_2$ cups oreo cookie crumbs
2 tablespoons melted butter or *for a non fat alternative, use prune puree*

FILLING

20 ounces low fat cream cheese, softened
1 cup sugar
1-$^1/_2$ teaspoon vanilla
4 eggs or 6 egg whites
10 squares semi-sweet chocolate, melted
$^1/_4$ cup Frangelico liqueur

Source: Kevan Thomas, Dessert Chef
Tomasitos, Santa Fe

1. Preheat oven to 325 degrees F.
2. Mix crumbs and melted butter for the crust. Press into bottom of 9 inch spring form pan. Bake 10 minutes.
3. Beat cream cheese, sugar and vanilla at medium speed until well blended, about 5 minutes. Add eggs, one at a time until well blended. Add in sour cream and melted chocolate and mix an additional 5 minutes. Add liqueur and beat 1 more minute. Pour over crust.
4. Bake 60 minutes or until center is set. Run metal spatula around rim of spring form pan to loosen cake, cool before removing rim of pan. Refrigerate 4 hours or overnight. Serve with Raspberry Creme Sauce.

RASPBERRY CREME SAUCE

$^1/_2$ quart heavy whipping cream
20 ounces fresh or frozen raspberries
$^1/_2$ cup powdered sugar
$^1/_2$ tablespoon cream of tartar
$^1/_2$ cup melted, but slightly cooled, white chocolate

Whip cream until stiff. Add powdered sugar and cream of tartar. In a blender, puree raspberries until smooth. Gently fold raspberries into whipping cream mixture. Gently fold melted, but cooled, white chocolate into raspberry cream mixture. Refrigerate immediately.

RASPBERRY MARBLE CAKE

This cake is very dramatic as a birthday cake, or for a special celebration cake. Instead of a glaze, you may choose to top with glaze and fresh raspberries or a fluffy icing.

1 cup fresh or frozen (thawed) raspberries
1 tablespoon sugar
$1/2$ cup reduced-fat margarine or *lite* **butter**
1 cup sugar
3 egg whites, beaten stiff
1 teaspoon almond extract
2 to 1-$1/2$ cups unbleached flour
$1/4$ cup oat bran
1-$1/4$ teaspoons baking soda
1-$1/4$ cups nonfat buttermilk

GLAZE:
$1/3$ cup powdered sugar
$1/4$ teaspoon almond extract
2 teaspoons nonfat buttermilk

1. Preheat oven to 350 degree F.
2. In a blender put the raspberries and sugar to puree. Put aside.
3. In a bowl combine the margarine and sugar. Use an electric mixer and beat until smooth. In another bowl, mix the flour, oat bran, and baking soda. Add the flour mixture and the buttermilk to the margarine mixture, and beat just until well mixed. Fold in egg whites.
4. Marbleize by removing $3/4$ cup of the batter, and mix with the raspberry puree. Put aside.
5. Spray a 12-cup bundt pan with vegetable oil. Spread $2/3$ of the plain batter evenly in the pan. Top with the raspberry batter, and follow with the remaining plain batter.
6. Bake for 35-40 minutes. Test with a wood pick for doneness. Cool the cake 10-15 minutes. Invert onto wire rack. Cool to room temperature.
7. Combine glaze ingredients and stir until smooth. Transfer the cake to serving platter, and drizzle the glaze over the cake.

RASPBERRY BAVARIAN CAKE (NON-FAT)

2 large packages raspberry jello
2 cups boiling water
1 cup evaporated skim milk
1 cup fresh raspberries or 10 oz. thawed and drained frozen raspberries
1 Angel cake, cut crossways into 3 layers

In shallow pan, freeze evaporated milk just until ice crystals form around edges. Dissolve gelatin in boiling water, chill until partially set. In a chilled mixing bowl, beat frosty milk with electric beater until stiff, then fold this into partially set jello. Then gently fold in raspberries. Frost cake layers with filling and stack. Frost entire cake with remaining raspberry frosting. Chill until set.

RASPBERRY-YOGURT PIE

This is almost a health food. It is perfect for those hot July evenings. Since this is the time when the raspberries are their best and most reasonably priced, summer is the time to make this nutritious creation.

Preparation tips: Because this recipe is for a 10 inch pie, if you use a smaller pie plate, you will find that you have extra filling. Put this in dessert glasses and have it with out a crust.

This pie can be made ahead two days since this filling will not fall or weep.

FILLING

4 cups fresh raspberries, rinsed and well drained
1/3 cup orange juice or apple juice
2 envelopes (2 scant tablespoons) unflavored gelatin
1/3 cup sugar
2 cups plain nonfat or low-fat yogurt
1 tablespoon honey (optional)
1 tablespoon raspberry vinegar or other mild, fruity vinegar
1/2 teaspoon vanilla extract

1. Preheat the oven to 350 degrees F.
2. To make the crust, in a small bowl, thoroughly combine the crust ingredients. Press them into a large pie plate, making sure that the sides are covered up to the rim of the plate.
3. Place the pie plate in the hot oven, and bake the crust for 10 to 15 minutes or until it is a light brown. Set the crust on a rack to cool before filling it.
4. To make the filling, select enough of the best raspberries to make 1 cup and set aside.
5. Place the orange or apple juice in a small bowl or measuring cup, and sprinkle in the gelatin. Let the mixture stand for 5 minutes or until the gelatin has softened.
6. In a small saucepan, combine 1 heaping cup of the remaining berries with the sugar. Cook the berries, stirring them, over a medium-low heat for 3 to 5 minutes or until the sugar dissolves. Remove the pan from the heat, and add the softened gelatin, stirring the ingredients until the gelatin is dissolved. Set the mixture aside to cool somewhat.
7. Add to a blender or food processor the yogurt, honey, vinegar, vanilla, and the raspberry-gelatin syrup, do not worry if it is still quite warm. Process the mixture until it is smooth and well blended. Place the remaining raspberries (not those that you are reserving in step 4) along the bottom of the cooled crust (the pie looks especially beautiful when sliced if you stand each berry on its rim with the hole side down). Spoon the yogurt mixture over the berries, and place the pie in the refrigerator for about 1 hour. Decorate the top of the pie with the reserved berries. An arrangement of the berries along the perimeter and a second circle of berries in the middle of the pie is a good look. Chill the pie for 2 hours or until it is very firm.

Here are three recipes for crusts, use one from the next page.

GRAHAM CRACKER CRUST
1-1/2 cups graham-cracker crumbs
1 tablespoon sugar (optional)
1/4 cup (1/2 stick) *lite* margarine, melted or if you wish, 1/4 cup canola oil

No-Fat Variation:

In food processor make crumbs of 8 crackers. Add 2 tablespoons of sugar and 2 tablespoons Prune Puree (page 15). Use a vegetable spray on the sides and bottom of pie pan. Bake at 350 degree F. for 10 minutes.

PECAN CRUST
8 ounces pecans, grind these but not until they become oily
1/4 cup sugar
3/8 teaspoon cardamom

To make graham cracker or pecan crust, preheat the oven to 400 degrees F. In a small bowl, combine the crust ingredients. Press the mixture onto the bottom and sides of a greased, 11 inch tart pan with a removable bottom. Place the pan in the hot oven, and bake the crust for 10 minutes or until the crust is firm and lightly browned on the edges. Place the crust on a rack to cool thoroughly before filling it.

LADYFINGER CRUST

Split 12 ladyfingers. Use some to line bottom of deep 9 inch pie pan. Cut some in half crosswise and arrange around edge of pan. Break remainder into small pieces and fill spaces in bottom of pan. Melt 2 tablespoons margarine; pour over ladyfingers in bottom. Chill.

RED RASPBERRY PIE

1 cup fresh raspberries
1 tablespoon lemon juice
1 cup sugar or honey
pinch sea salt
1/3 cup Creme de Cassis
2 tablespoons unsalted butter
4 tablespoons cornstarch
3 paper thin slices lemon

Combine berries and sugar in mixing bowl. Whisk Cassis and cornstarch until smooth, add lemon juice and salt and stir gently into berries. Line 9 inch pie plate with pastry. Spoon in berries, dot with butter, arrange lemon slices (over lapping slightly) in center. Top with lattice crust. Bake in center of oven, 425 degrees F. for 15 minutes, then 350 degrees F. for 30-40 minutes.

Variation: To one quart of raspberries add 2-1/2 tablespoons cornstarch, 1/2 cup water, 1/2 cup orange juice cooked over low heat, stirring constantly, until thick (10-15 minutes). Add 1 cup of pureed raspberries. Put the 3 cups of whole raspberries in pie shell. Pour syrup over the berries and chill in refrigerator 4-5 hours.

RASPBERRY CHEESECAKE PIE

CRUST
3/4 cup vanilla wafers
1/2 cup rolled oats
1/2 cup pecans or walnuts
1/4 cup melted butter, margarine, or canola oil

FILLING
1 8-ounce package cream cheese
1 8-ounce nonfat cottage cheese
1/2 cup sugar
1/2 teaspoon vanilla
Dash salt
2 whole eggs plus 3 whites

RASPBERRY GLAZE TOPPING:
2 cups fresh raspberries
1/2 cup of orange or lemon juice
1 teaspoon plus 1 tablespoons cornstarch
1/2 cup sugar

Combine crumbs and butter; press into oiled 8 inch pie plate, building up sides. Beat softened cream cheese till fluffy; gradually blend in 1/2 cup sugar, lemon juice, vanilla, and salt. Add eggs one at a time, beating well after each. Pour filling into crumb crust. Bake in slow oven, 325 degrees F., 25 to 30 minutes or until set.

Crush 1 cup of raspberries; add the water, and cook 2 minutes; sieve. Mix cornstarch with sugar (amount of sugar depends on sweetness of berries); stir into hot berry mixture. Bring to boiling point, stirring constantly. Cook and stir until thick and clear. Cool to room temperature. Place cool raspberries on top cool cheesecake.

To reduce fat: Use nonfat cream cheese and 15 ounces nonfat ricotta cheese, 1/2 cup fat-free egg substitute and the Prune Pie Crust.

RASPBERRY CHIFFON PIE

Makes one 9-inch pie, adapted from the Woman's Day Kitchen

1 box raspberry-flavored gelatin
2/3 cup boiling water
1/8 teaspoon salt (optional)
2 tablespoons lemon juice
1 box (10-oz.) frozen raspberries, thawed
3 egg whites
1/3 cup sugar
Ladyfinger Crust, Pecan Crust or Graham Cracker Crust

Dissolve gelatin in boiling water. Add salt, lemon juice, and raspberries. Chill until thickened, but not firm. Beat egg whites until foamy; gradually add sugar, and beat until stiff, but not dry. Fold into gelatin. Fill up crust; chill until firm.

CLAFOUTI-AUX FRAMBOISES

1 egg yolk or ¹/₄ cup egg substitute
1 whole egg or substitute
¹/₄ cup plus 2 tablespoons flour
¹/₂ cup sugar
6 tablespoons *lite* margarine or softened butter
³/₄ cup milk
1-³/₄ cups fresh raspberries
1-¹/₂ tablespoons Kirsch, or same amount of an orange liqueur

Preheat oven 400 degrees F. Using an electric blender combine the egg, flour, milk, Kirsch, butter and sugar. Blend until smooth. Spray a 9-inch pie plate or quiche pan. Pour half of the batter in the pie or quiche plate. Sprinkle raspberries over the batter and spread the remaining 2 tablespoons sugar over top. Pour the remaining batter over the raspberries and sugar. Bake until the batter puffs up and is lightly brown, approximately 45 minutes. The cleft will sink as it cools, therefore is best eaten warm. You may need to cool it, then reheat to serve at a later time.

Yield: *6-8 servings*

WHATZABERRY PIE

Make this pie with a Prune Pie Crust and it will be nutritious, versatile and delicious. The name implies that you can use different kinds of berries, black berries, Himalayan, boysenberries, gooseberries and so on. Use seasonally, local fresh berries and or even 1 cup of cherries as one of the choices.

¹/₄ cup sugar
¹/₄ cup of cornstarch
1 cup raspberry juice blend, such as cran-raspberry
1 cup nonfat raspberry yogurt
1 cup fresh raspberries
2 cups any other fresh berries, like blueberries and strawberries
Prune Pie Crust

In a medium sized saucepan, combine the sugar and cornstarch. Slowly add the juice. Stir in the yogurt. Bring the mixture to a boil using medium heat and stirring with a wire whisk. Stirring constantly, reduce the heat to low and cook for an additional 2 minutes. Let the mixture cool for 15 minutes. Gently stir the fruits together. Pour a thin layer of the fruit mixture over bottom of pie crust. Top it with half of the fruit and half of remaining filling. Repeat, ending with the filling. Cool for 4-6 hours, until the filling is set. Serve cold.

Yield: *Serves 8*

COOKIES

FAT PROBLEMS WITH MOST COOKIES

In almost any cookie recipe there are high calories, and high fat, that converts to body fat when eaten. Here's an example of sugar cookies' ingredients:

Ingredient	Calories	Fat
2 cups flour	800	4.5 grams
1 cup sugar	720	0 grams
1 cup butter	1,600	177 grams
2 eggs	150	10 grams

Nuts contain about 800 calories and 70 grams of fat. The fat in nuts is mostly unsaturated and does not raise blood cholesterol levels. Since the Raspberry Fruit Balls have no butter or sugar, it is not only reduced in fat and calories, but they are nutritious! Try them as a delicious, low-fat substitute.

RASPBERRY & DRIED FRUIT BALLS

This recipe is adapted from "Your Kitchen" of Woman's Day Gifts.

1¹/₂ cups dried raspberries (see General Information section)
1 cup dried apricots
1 cup pitted dates
³/₄ cup raisins
¹/₂ cup grated carrots
1 cup coconut flakes (preferably unsweetened)
¹/₂ cup powdered sugar
2 tablespoons orange juice or orange liqueur
Optional: Ground nuts (walnuts, hazelnuts, or pecans)
         Grated semi-sweet chocolate

1. In a chopping bowl or food processor, chop the apricots, dates, raisins and coconut. Stir in raspberries, carrots, juice or liqueur, mixing the ingredients thoroughly.

2. Spoon off enough of the mixture to shape into 1 inch balls (first dusting with powdered sugar, if necessary). Cool the fruit balls in the chocolate or ground nuts. Place the balls in a layered fashion in a tightly covered container. Separate the layers with paper.

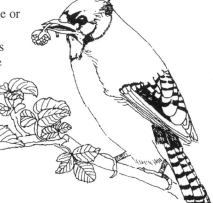

RASPBERRY FIRECRACKERS

For a simple stuffing, fill each wonton skin with three, small, whole raspberries.

¹/₂ pint fresh raspberries
2 ounces semi-sweet chocolate, finely grated
1 tablespoon finely grated orange zest
36 wonton skins
3 cups vegetable oil (canola) for frying
1 tablespoon confectioners sugar
Ginger Caramel Sauce

1. In a small bowl, toss the raspberries with the chocolate, sugar and orange zest.

2. Place 1 wonton skin on a work surface, keep the remaining skins covered. Place ¹/₂ teaspoon of the filling in one corner of the wonton skin, roll up diagonally to tightly enclose the filling. Twist the ends in opposite directions and pinch together to form a "firecracker". Repeat the procedure with the remaining skins and filling.

3. In a medium skillet, heat the oil to 375 degrees F. Fry the firecrackers in batches of 4 at a time, until lightly browned, about 1 minute. With a slotted spoon, transfer them to paper towels to drain and cool slightly.

4. Dust the firecrackers with confectioners sugar and serve warm on their own or with the Ginger Caramel Sauce.

Yield: About 36 firecrackers

GINGER CARAMEL SAUCE

This sauce is also good with pound cake, bread pudding and ice cream.

¹/₂ cup and 2 tablespoons heavy cream
2 teaspoons grated fresh ginger
1 cup sugar
1 teaspoon fresh lemon juice

1. In a small saucepan, simmer ¹/₂ cup of heavy cream with the ginger for about 10 minutes. Set aside.

2. In another small heavy saucepan, cook the sugar with the more juice over low heat, stirring frequently, until the sugar caramelizes to a light brown color, 10 to 15 minutes. Being careful to avoid splatters, stir in the remaining 2 tablespoons heavy cream. Remove from heat.

3. Strain the ginger cream into a bowl and whisk in the caramel cream until smooth. Serve warm.

The sauce will keep refrigerated for up to 1 month. Rewarm over low heat before serving.

Yield: About 1 cup

HAZELNUT RASPBERRY-FILLED THUMB PRINT COOKIES

This is a cookie that I make at Christmas and I use preserves that I have made in the summer, but there is no reason that you cannot make them in the summer when you have children at home with nothing to do. Kids love to make the thumb print, and mine love to pick the raspberries. If they had cookies to put the berries into perhaps they wouldn't eat all they pick in the patch! The cookies only take 15 minutes to prepare and 15 minutes to bake so it is a fast, nutritious and fun cookie.

2 cups whole wheat pastry flour
1 cup ground hazelnuts
2 teaspoons baking powder
1/4 teaspoon sea salt
1/3 cup canola oil or melted *lite* margarine
1/3 cup orange juice
1/3 cup maple syrup or concentrated fruit sweetener
1-1/2 teaspoons almond extract
1/2 teaspoon vanilla
Raspberry preserves

1. Preheat oven to 350 degrees F. Combine flour, hazelnuts, baking powder and salt in a mixing bowl.

2. In a separate bowl, mix oil, juice, syrup, almond and vanilla extracts together. Add wet ingredients to dry and mix well, kneading a little.

3. Use a tablespoon to scoop dough and form into balls. Flatten into circles. Place on lightly oiled or parchment-lined cookie sheet. Indent each cookie with your thumb and put 1/2 teaspoon preserves in the imprint. Bake 15 minutes or until edges turn golden.

Yield: *2 dozen cookies*

CHOCOLATE RASPBERRY TRUFFLES

These are rich and irresistible. They are hardly a cookie, but we will disguise-name them as such, so you won't feel so sinful when you are eating them. After a special large meal, they are a tiny treat that every guest will try. The outside coating can be done in many ways, limited only by imagination - dried raspberries, unsweetened cocoa powder, powdered sugar, white chocolate, nuts, etc.

1/4 pint heavy cream (2/3 cup)
9 ounces bitter or semi-sweet (plain) chocolate, broken into pieces
2 tablespoons raspberry jam or raspberry syrup
3 tablespoons cocoa powder

1. Pour the cream into a heavy pan and bring to a boil. Remove from the heat and add the chocolate. Stir until melted and well blended. Stir in the raspberry jam. Set aside to cool, then chill for at least 1 hour.

2. Using a melon "baller" with a 3/4 inch scoop, or 2 small teaspoons, form the mixture into balls and place them on a baking sheet lined with non-stick baking paper. Chill for 1 hour.

3. Sift 3 tbsps. cocoa into small bowl. Roll the truffles in the cocoa to coat them on all sides, turning them over and over with a wooden cocktail stick or toothpick. It is not customary to make the truffles perfectly round. Place them in small paper cases and store them in a box in the refrigerator. Remove them about 30 minutes before serving.

RASPBERRY FILLED PASTRY TRIANGLES

6 ounces *lite* margarine, chilled
2 ounces prune butter
1 egg
2-1/2 to 3 cups flour
3 tablespoons sugar
12 ounces raspberries (6 oz. fresh plus 6 oz. jam)
Vegetable oil spray

1. Combine in a large mixing bowl or food processor the chilled margarine, prune butter and sugar. Using fingertips, mix the ingredients until it looks like coarse meal. Continue to mix and beat eggs into dough until smooth. Make a ball and wrap it in wax paper and chill for 1 hour, or until the dough is very hard.

2. Heat the preserves, stirring constantly over moderate heat for 3 to 5 minutes or until very thin. Cool. Add fresh raspberries.

3. Cut the cold dough into halves. Shape each half into rectangles. Roll each half between two sheets of floured wax paper. Roll both layers of dough approximately 10 x 15 inches long. Remove wax paper from both layers placing one on a cookie sheet and other on smooth non-lipped surface so it can slide off easily.

4. Using vegetable spray, coat the cookie sheet. Spread the raspberry mixture on top of the first layer. Using a hard background under the second dough layer, place on top of the dough topped with raspberries. In a 250 degrees F. oven, bake 55 minutes, or until the pastry begins to turn a pale gold. Watch carefully for any sign of burning, and adjust the heat downward.

ICING
2 cups powdered sugar
2 teaspoons lemon juice
1/4 cup raspberry juice

Stir the sugar, water and lemon juice in a large bowl to make a thin icing. Spread over the top layer of pastry with a spatula and set pastry sheet aside to cool. Slice with a sharp knife into triangles or strips.

Yield: about 4 dozen

Put the first layer of dough on a cookie sheet and top with raspberry filling

Using a non-lipped, smooth surface, slide the second layer of dough onto the first layer

Bake and cool before slicing and/or icing triangles. Be very careful when lifting off the cookie sheet!

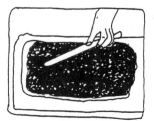
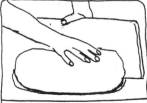

RASPBERRY CRESCENTS

1 cup flour
3 ounces cream cheese, softened
$1/2$ cup *lite* margarine
$1/4$ cup raspberry jam or preserves

1. Combine flour, cream cheese and margarine and knead with hands to form dough. Divide dough in half and shape each half into a ball. Wrap and chill overnight.
2. On lightly floured surface, roll out each ball to about a 9 inch circle. Cut each into 12 wedges. Put $1/2$ teaspoon raspberry jam on wide end of each wedge. Roll toward point and shape into crescent. Place point down on oiled cookie sheet.
3. Bake in preheated 400 degrees F. for 10 to 15 minutes of until golden brown. Cool on rack. Frost. Store airtight in cool place for 10 days. Can be frozen up to 6 months.

FROSTING
2 tablespoons pistachios
$1/2$ cup confectioner sugar
2+ teaspoons lemon juice

Blend sugar with lemon juice. Use enough juice to make a thin frosting. Drizzle crescents with frosting and sprinkle with pistachios.

Yield: 2 dozen

CHOCOBERRY COOKIES

4 tablespoons *lite* margarine or butter
$3/4$ cup brown sugar
$1/4$ cup chocolate syrup
1 tablespoon plus 1 teaspoon water
1 teaspoon vanilla extract
1-$1/2$ cups whole wheat flour
1 cup quick cooking oats
2 tablespoons cocoa powder
$3/4$ teaspoon baking soda
3 tablespoons + 1-$1/2$ teaspoons raspberry fruit spread or jam

1. Preheat oven to 300 degrees F. In a blender or bowl, combine margarine and sugar until smooth. Mix the chocolate, water and vanilla and blend until smooth.
2. Combine the flour, oats, cocoa and baking soda in a separate bowl.
3. Add the margarine to the flour mixture and blend until the dough comes away from the side of the bowl. Make a ball with the dough.
4. Oil the baking sheet with vegetable spray. Roll the dough to form 1 inch balls and place the balls on the cookie sheet. If the dough is sticky, place it in the freezer for a few minutes. Space the balls 1-$1/2$ inches apart. Use the back of a $1/4$ inch measuring teaspoon to make the depression that will hold the jam in the cookies. To keep the measuring spoon from sticking, dip it in sugar. Fill the depression with $1/2$ teaspoon of fruit spread. Bake cookies approximately 20 minutes until nicely browned. Store in air tight container.

RASPBERRY WALNUT SNOW BARS

1-1/4 cups + 2 tablespoons sifted flour
1/2 cup sugar
1/2 cup butter
1/3 cup raspberry jam
2 eggs
1/2 cup firmly packed brown sugar
1/2 teaspoon vanilla extract
1/8 teaspoon baking soda
Pinch salt
1 cup chopped walnuts

1. Preheat oven to 350 degrees F. Combine flour and sugar. Cut in butter until mixture is like fine meal. Press into lightly oiled 9 inch square baking dish. Bake 20 minutes until edges turn light brown. Remove from oven and cover crust with raspberry jam.

2. Beat eggs with brown sugar and vanilla until well blended. Stir in 2 tablespoons flour, pinch salt and baking soda. Add walnuts and mix. Spoon over jam and spread lightly to corners of pan. Return pan to oven and bake additional 20-25 minutes or until topping is set. Cool in pan and cut into 18 squares.

CHOCOLATE TOPPING
1 square unsweetened chocolate
1 tablespoon margarine
1 cup confectioners sugar
pinch salt
1/2 teaspoon vanilla
1 - 2 tablespoons water

Melt chocolate and margarine over low heat, stirring constantly until smooth. Remove from heat. Stir in sugar, salt, and enough water to make mixture spreadable. Spread onto cooled bars.

Yield: *18 bars*

BERRY SORBET

2 cups each blackberries and raspberries, rinsed and drained
Additional blackberries and raspberries, rinsed and drained (optional)
1-1/2 cups powdered fructose
1/2 cup water
2 tablespoons lime juice
Black raspberry-flavor liqueur
Fresh mint sprigs, for garnish

In a 2-3 quart pan, combine the 2 cups blackberries, 2 cups raspberries, fructose, water and lime juice. Bring to a boil over high heat, stirring often. Then reduce heat and simmer until blackberries mash readily, 3 to 4 minutes. Blend mixture a portion at a time, in a blender or food processor until pureed. To remove seeds, put puree through fine strainer into a bowl.

Pour puree into a 9 to 10-inch square metal pan. Cover airtight and freeze until firm, at least 8 hours or up to 2 weeks.

Frozen sorbet has an icy texture. If you like a softer texture, break down frozen sorbet into chunks and beat with a mixer until slushy; serve at once or return to freezer up to 1 hour. Top with servings of sorbet with additional berries and a mint sprig.

WATERMELON & RASPBERRY SORBET

1 cup water
2/3 cup sugar
2-3/4 pound piece of watermelon, rind and seeds discarded, flesh cut into chunks (4-1/2 cups)
4 teaspoons fresh lemon juice
1 cup fresh raspberries

In a saucepan, simmer water with sugar, stirring until sugar dissolves. In a blender puree watermelon, sugar syrup, lemon juice, and 1/2 cup raspberries and strain through a fine sieve into a bowl, pressing hard on solids. Chill mixture, covered, until cold, about 2 hours. Freeze mixture in an ice-cream maker. Serve scoop garnished with remaining 1/2 cup raspberries. Sorbet may be made 1 week ahead.

Yield: about 5 cups

RASPBERRY & WHITE WINE SORBET

Call it sorbet or call it fruit ice, this is a zesty dessert, especially when a little Cream de Cassis is drizzled over each serving! It helps the raspberry flavor, with its winy undertone, and is marvelously enhanced by the black-currant liqueur. Served in small portions without the cassis topping, the ice is also appropriate as a palate-refresher midway through a multi-course dinner. Unlike many ices, this one keeps its silky texture for up to 2 weeks in the freezer.

3 cups fresh raspberries, picked over, rinsed and drained if necessary
1-1/3 cups sugar
2/3 cup water
1-1/2 cups dry white wine
1/4 cup Creme de Cassis (optional)

1. Puree raspberries in food processor or blender until smooth. Press puree through fine-mesh sieve with back of spoon to remove seeds; discard seeds.
2. Heat sugar and 2/3 cup water in small saucepan to boiling; boil, uncovered, until mushy, about 3 minutes. Remove from heat; stir in wine and optional Creme de Cassis; let cool.
3. Stir raspberry puree into cooled wine mixture. Pour mixture into 8 or 9-inch shallow metal pan. Freeze, uncovered, until mushy, about 3 hours.

Yield: About 1-1/2 pints

FROZEN RASPBERRY CREME

1 egg white, beaten stiff
1 cup of whipping cream (or non-fat yogurt)
1/4 cup confectioners sugar
1/2 teaspoon vanilla

Line a 3-pint melon mold with Raspberry Ice, recipe below. Fill the center with whipped cream or yogurt, to which the other ingredients have been added. Let stand packed in equal parts of ice and salt for 3 hours.

RASPBERRY ICE
4 cups water
2 cups berry juice
1-1/2 cups sugar
1 tablespoon lemon juice
Make a syrup of sugar and water, and boil 10 minutes; cool, add berry juice and lemon juice; strain and freeze.

RASPBERRY RHAPSODY

Very rich! Vary the portions with the guests capacities!

1 pt. heavy cream or non-fat yogurt
1-1/2 cups confectioners sugar
6 teaspoons of orange liqueur or sherry
1/4 cup shaved dark chocolate or chopped maraschino cherries
1/2 cup chopped pecans
1 quart raspberry sherbet
Rhapsody Sauce

Whip cream (yogurt) adding sifted sugar, liquor, shaved chocolate and pecans. Pour half this mixture into a 9 inch square pan. Spread 1 quart sherbet over mixture. Add the remaining half of mixture. Freeze for 24 hours. Top with the below Rhapsody Sauce.

RHAPSODY SAUCE:
2 boxes frozen raspberries
1/2 cup sugar
4 tablespoons water
4 teaspoons lemon juice
6 tablespoons orange liqueur or sherry

Add all the ingredients, except the liqueur, in a pan and boil for 5 minutes. Add the liqueur and boil just long enough to remove the alcohol. Remove the frozen cream mixture from the freezer about 15 minutes before serving. Have sauce at room temperature and pour it over each square cut portion.

FROZEN RASPBERRY YOGURT

2 pints fresh raspberries
1 cup sugar
2 cups plain low-fat yogurt (optional no-fat)
Fresh mint sprigs for garnish

In a blender or food processor, puree the raspberries with the sugar. Pass the puree through a fine sieve. In a bowl, whisk the yogurt until smooth and stir in the raspberry puree. Pour the mixture into an ice cream maker and freeze according to manufacturer's instructions. Transfer the frozen yogurt to a container and freeze until firm. Spoon the yogurt into tall glasses, garnish with mint sprigs and serve.

FROZEN RASPBERRY YOGURT PIE

One graham cracker pie crust, with a $1/2$ cup of pecan pieces sprinkled on the bottom
1-8 ounce cream cheese
1 cup Frozen Raspberry Yogurt
1 teaspoon vanilla
4 to 6 tablespoons honey

Mix softened cream cheese (optional lowered -fat cream cheese), the Frozen Raspberry Yogurt, vanilla, and honey (to taste). Mix all together. Put into pie shell, chill and serve with raspberries.

EASY RASPBERRY ICE CREAM

This is not only easy, and nutritious but it is low in fat, freezes smooth and without stirring.

1 egg separated
$1/2$ cup Pet instant milk (in dry form)
$1/3$ cup water
$1/3$ cup sugar
3 tablespoons lemon juice
10-oz. pkg. frozen raspberries, thawed

With an electric mixer at high speed, beat 1 egg white, Pet instant milk (in dry form) and water in a small mixing bowl or 1-1/2 qt. bowl until stiff. Beat in gradually sugar and lemon juice until very stiff. Beat in egg yolk just until mixed. Fold in 10-oz. pkg. frozen raspberries, thawed. Freeze in ice trays.

Yield: 6 -7 servings

BANANA & RASPBERRY ICE CREAM

Mashed bananas give this icy creation is creamy consistency. Garnish with raspberries.

4 bananas
$3/4$ cup one percent light soy milk
$1/2$ cup frozen raspberries, thawed and drained
$1/2$ cup unsweetened apple juice

Peel and slice bananas and puree with remaining ingredients in a food processor. Freeze mixture in an ice cream maker according to manufacturer's instructions.

Preparation time: 5 minutes   Freezing time: 1 hour and 30 minutes

RICH RASPBERRY ICE CREAM

The ultimate in raspberries and cream! An ice cream fruity and rich enough to inspire a *"come-for dessert party"*. This particular recipe requires no cooking, but allow time for the overnight mellowing of the raspberries and sugar mixture. Raspberries vary considerably in tartness, so taste the mixture of fruit and cream before freezing and add more sugar if necessary. Like all fine homemade ice creams, this should be enjoyed at its best, within a day or so of being prepared.

3 cups fresh raspberries, picked over, rinsed and drained if necessary
1 cup sugar, or more if needed
2 cups heavy cream, preferably not ultra-pasteurized
1 cup milk
2 teaspoons vanilla

1. Place raspberries in a large bowl, sprinkle with 1 cup sugar. Stir, crushing raspberries slightly with back of large spoon. Refrigerate mixture, covered at least 6 hours or overnight, stirring occasionally.

2. Strain raspberries through medium-mesh sieve, catching juices in a bowl. Press raspberries very lightly with the back of spoon to extract juices; do not crush raspberries completely. Transfer raspberry pulp to separate bowl; refrigerate, covered. Stir heavy cream, milk, and vanilla into raspberry juice.

3. Freeze cream mixture in ice-cream freezer, following manufacturer's directions, until ice cream is ready to pack and harden in your freezer. Stir reserved raspberry pulp into ice-cream mixture. Resume freezing, running the machine a few minutes longer, or until ice cream again reaches the desired consistency for packing and freezing. Pack ice cream into freezer container or containers; cover tightly. Place in freezer until ice cream is firm, at least 3 hours or longer.

4. Scrape ice cream into food processor or large bowl of electric mixer; process or beat until fluffy, working quickly to prevent excessive melting. Scrape mixture back into metal pan; cover tightly with aluminum foil. Freeze until firm, about 3 hours longer.

5. At serving time, scoop into chilled dessert glasses. Serve immediately.

Tips: Additional Creme de Cassis can be used as a topping, if desired. Sorbet can be stored tightly covered, in freezer up to 2 weeks.

Yield: *about 2 quarts*

CHOCOLATE-RASPBERRY JAM BREAD PUDDING

No one will guess there's tofu in this decadent dessert made with chocolate chips and raspberry jam.

2 10.5-ounce boxes silken *lite* firm tofu
1/3 cup granulated cane or fruit juice sweetener
1/2 cup *lite* soy milk
1 tablespoon cinnamon
1/4 teaspoon ground nutmeg
1/4 teaspoon salt (optional)
1/8 teaspoon ground cardamom
1 teaspoon vanilla extract
2 egg whites or equivalent egg replacer
5 cups day-old crusty whole-grain French bread cubes
1/2 cup chocolate or carob chips
1/3 cup all-fruit raspberry jam

1. Preheat oven to 350 degrees F. Spray a 1-1/2 quart baking dish with vegetable cooking spray.

2. In a blender or food processor, combine tofu, sweetener, soy milk, spices, salt, vanilla and egg whites until smooth.

3. Place half the bread cubes in prepared baking dish. Cover with half of the tofu mixture, half of the chocolate chips and half of the jam.

4. Layer remaining bread, tofu mixture, chocolate chips and jam in dish.

5. Bake in oven for 1 hour or until set in center. Serve slightly warm topped with soymilk or tofu whipped cream.

GRILLED PEACHES WITH RASPBERRY PUREE

1/2 (10 ounce) package frozen raspberries in light syrup, slightly thawed
1-1/2 teaspoons lemon juice
2 medium ripe peaches, peeled, halved, and pitted
1-1/2 tablespoons brown sugar
1/4 teaspoon ground cinnamon (cardamom optional)
1-1/2 teaspoons rum flavoring (orange liqueur option)
1-1/2 teaspoons margarine

Recipe by Barbara Valdez

1. Combine raspberries and lemon juice in electric blender or food processor and process until smooth. Strain raspberry puree; discard seeds. Cover and chill.

2. Cut 1 (18 x18 inch) sheet of heavy-duty aluminum foil. Place peach halves, cut side up, on foil. Combine brown sugar and cinnamon; spoon evenly into center of each peach half.

3. Sprinkle with rum flavoring, and dot with margarine. Fold foil over peaches, and loosely seal.

4. Place grill rack over medium coals; place peach bundle on rack, and cook 15 minutes or until peaches are thoroughly heated.

5. To serve, spoon 2 tablespoons raspberry puree over each grilled peach half.

Yield: 4 servings (about 99 calories per serving)

RASPBERRY-RICOTTA PUDDING

This artery-sparing but rich tasting, pudding is a winner. It is a spectacular cross between a souffle and a cheesecake. NOTE: It is important that the ricotta must be drained overnight. The pudding and sauce can be prepared ahead and chilled, but bring the pudding to room temperature before serving it.

SAUCE

12 ounces frozen unsweetened raspberries, thawed, with their juice reserved
3 tablespoons sugar
1 tablespoon fresh lemon juice

PUDDING

2 15-ounce containers *lite* or part-skim ricotta
1/3 cup plus 1 tablespoon sugar, divided
1 egg yolk (reserve the white)
1 teaspoon lemon extract or lemon juice
1 teaspoon lemon peel
1/4 teaspoon cinnamon
3 tablespoons all-purpose flour
2 egg whites, at room temperature
pinch salt
Vegetable-oil spray
1 pint fresh raspberries for garnish

1. To make the sauce, in a food processor, blender, or food mill, puree the raspberries with the sugar and lemon juice.
2. Strain the mixture through a fine sieve onto a bowl to remove the seeds, pressing on the solids to retrieve as much of the pulp as possible. Cover the bowl, and refrigerate the sauce until serving time.
3. To make the pudding, place the ricotta in a sieve set over a bowl. Cover the bowl, and refrigerate the ricotta overnight.
4. In a food processor or blender, puree the drained ricotta with the 1/3 cup of sugar, egg yolk, vanilla extract, almond extract, and cinnamon. Continue processing the ingredients for 5 minutes or until the mixture is light though grainy. Transfer the mixture to a large bowl. Fold in the flour, lemon juice, and lemon peel.
5. Preheat the oven to 350 degrees F.
6. In a medium-sized bowl, beat the egg whites with the salt until they form soft peaks. Gradually add the 1 tablespoon of sugar, and continue beating the egg whites until they are stiff but not dry. Gently fold the beaten egg whites into the ricotta mixture.
7. Spray a 1-3/4 quart baking dish with vegetable oil. Spoon the ricotta mixture into the dish. Set the dish in a larger pan, and pour enough boiling water into the larger pan so that the water reaches halfway up the sides of the smaller baking dish.
8. Place the pudding in the hot oven, and bake the pudding for 45 minutes or until the pudding is puffed and golden. Remove the pudding from the outer pan, and place it on a rack to cool to room temperature. Serve the pudding garnished with raspberries and topped with the sauce.

RASPBERRY CREAM

2 cups whipping cream or non-fat vanilla yogurt
1 cup low fat milk
$1/2$ cup sugar
$1/4$ teaspoon salt
2 envelopes unflavored gelatin
2 tablespoons water
2 cups nonfat sour cream
1 teaspoon vanilla extract
1 cup raspberries

1. Heat cream or yogurt, milk, sugar, and salt in a large saucepan until lukewarm. Stir until sugar dissolves.

2. Dissolve gelatin in cold water and set over hot water until clear. Add to cream mixture. When the mixture has cooled and is beginning to congeal, add vanilla and fold in sour cream. Pour into a mold or 9-inch pan. Chill and serve with Raspberries Sauce.

CRAN-RASPBERRY TOFU DESSERT

1 10-$1/2$ ounces package tofu, drained
1 teaspoon grated lemon zest
$1/2$ cup jellied cranberry sauce
$1/2$ cup raspberries
2 teaspoons lemon juice

Mix cranberry sauce and raspberries together. Combine rest of ingredients in blender or food processor until smooth, saving a teaspoon of cran-raspberry sauce for garnish, if desired. Chill. Serve. Garnish with fresh or frozen berry sauce, frozen yogurt, etc.

Yield: 3 servings

BERRY-BERRY CRUNCH

2 cups Quick Three Berry Cherry Sauce (see page 44)
1 cup fresh raspberries
1-1/2 cups whole wheat flour
1 teaspoon baking powder
1 egg or 2 egg whites
3/4 cup skim milk
1/2 cup chopped nuts
1/4 cup brown sugar
1/2 teaspoon lemon zest
1/4 cup firm margarine or butter

1. Preheat oven to 375 degrees F.
2. Mix the three berry mixture, and half of the raspberries in an ungreased square baking dish, 8 x12 inch; spread evenly.
3. Mix dry ingredients; flour, baking powder, sugar, nuts, and lemon zest together. Cut in margarine until crumbly; sprinkle over the berry mixture. Bake until brown, about 35 minutes. Serve with vanilla ice cream, or frozen yogurt if desired.

Yield: 6 to 8 servings

RASPBERRY CRISP

You will enjoy this, nutritious, easy to put together dessert. It is a recipe that you can get creative with, adding different things to the topping according to your taste.

3 cups raspberries
1 cup applesauce
1 teaspoon orange or lemon zest
2 egg whites or 1 whole egg, beaten lightly
1/2 cup brown sugar
1/2 cup whole wheat flour

TOPPING:

1/4 cup rolled oats
1/4 cup whole-wheat flour
1/4 cup powdered nonfat milk
1/4 cup packed brown sugar
1 teaspoon cardamom
1/4 teaspoon orange peel
2 tablespoons *lite* margarine
1/2 cup hazelnut, or walnut, pieces (optional)

1. *Important:* Preheat the oven to 375 degrees F. Mix the first 6 ingredients in a large bowl. Pour into a square baking dish, 3 x 10 x 12- inch oiled pan.
2. Combine the oats, flour, powdered milk, brown sugar, and spices, stirring the ingredients to mix them thoroughly. Now add the margarine, and mix until what you have looks like coarse meal. Stir in the chopped nuts. Sprinkle this mixture over the fruit. Bake for 35-40 minutes in a hot oven.

Yield: 6-8 servings

RASPBERRY TRIFLE (LOW-FAT)

This is an easy, light, good looking dessert, that looks and tastes delicious. It can be made 4 hours ahead and stored in the freezer. You will need to take it out one hour before serving and put it in the refrigerator.

1 small angel food cake (about 8-12 ounce)
1-1/2 cups raspberries unsweetened, frozen and unthawed
1/2 cup sugar depending on sweetness of berries
1/3 cup orange liqueur
1 teaspoon lemon or orange zest
2 cups vanilla frozen yogurt or 1 package lemon or vanilla low-fat pudding mix or
  Light Vanilla Custard (recipe follows)

1. Mix the orange liqueur, lemon zest, sugar and raspberries together in a small bowl.

2. Cut the angel food cake into 1/2 -3/4 inch slices for layering.

3. Using a lovely 2 quart, see-through glass, dessert bowl, put a layer of angel food cake on the bottom. Put 1/2 cup of the raspberry-sugar mix on the cake so that it can bleed through and tint the angel food cake pink.

4. Now layer 1/3 of the pudding, vanilla custard or frozen yogurt on top of the berry mixture.

5. Repeat this layering two more times, using all the ingredients.

6. Garnish top of trifle with fresh raspberries, if possible.

7. Keep frozen until one hour before serving. Keep chilled in the refrigerator until serving.

LIGHT VANILLA CUSTARD

2 tablespoons cornstarch
1/4 cup granulated sugar
1 egg yolk or 1 1/2 tablespoons egg substitute
1-1/2 cups nonfat milk
1 tablespoon unsalted butter or margarine
1-1/4 teaspoons vanilla extract

In a small saucepan blend the cornstarch with the sugar. Whisk in milk and blend. Over medium heat, bring to a boil. Whisk for about 30 seconds more, then remove from heat. Beat egg yolk until smooth. Whisk 1 cup of hot cornstarch mixture with the egg yolks; whisk back into remaining cornstarch mixture in saucepan. Cook over medium heat, whisking constantly, 30 seconds longer. Remove from heat and whisk in margarine or butter until melted. Pour into medium bowl; blend in vanilla. Let stand until slightly cooled, whisking several times. Cover with sheet of wax paper placed directly on custard and refrigerate until chilled before layering on the trifle.

RASPBERRY TRIFLES

3 eggs separated
1-1/3 cups Eagle Band Sweetened Condensed Milk (1 can)
1/2 cup lemon juice
1/4 teaspoon cream of tartar
1/4 cup sugar
1-1/2 cups (4-oz.) shredded coconut
1 package (10-oz) frozen raspberries, thawed and drained
8 baked tart shells, cooled

Beat egg yolks until thick and lemon colored. Gradually add Eagle Brand Milk while continuing to beat. Add lemon juice; blend well. Beat egg whites and cream of tartar until soft peaks form; gradually beat in sugar. Fold into lemon mixture. Gently fold in 1 cup coconut and drained raspberries. Spoon into shells. Sprinkle with remaining coconut. Garnish with whole raspberries. Chill.

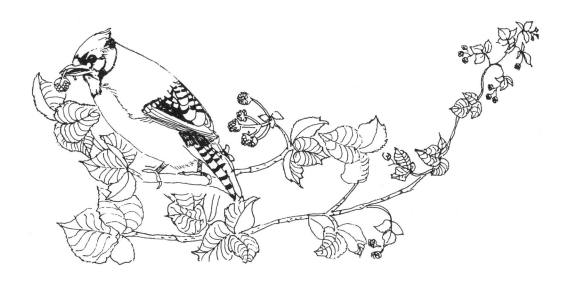

MOLDED RASPBERRY BAVARIAN CREAM

This recipe is located here because it too could be used in the trifle in place of the frozen yogurt or vanilla custard. It can be the filling for tarts or pie shells or can be a special dessert prepared in a mold, in a fluted ring mold or Bundt pan.

4 cups fresh raspberries, picked over, rinsed and drained if necessary
1-3/4 cups superfine sugar
2 tablespoons strained fresh lemon juice
4 teaspoons unflavored gelatin
1/2 cup cold water
1-1/2 cups heavy cream, cold

1. Set aside one cup of raspberries for garnish. In a food blender, puree the remainder of berries. Put berries through a sieve and use the juice or keep berries whole as you prefer. If you sieve them, you will have 1 cup of puree. Stir the raspberries or puree with sugar and lemon juice into strained puree until completely dissolved.

2. Sprinkle gelatin over 1/3 cup cold water in small saucepan. Let stand only until softened, about 5 minutes. Heat over very low heat, stirring constantly, until gelatin is dissolved. Do not allow to boil. Remove from heat, stir in raspberries.

3. Fill a large pan with ice and add 1 cup of cold water. Put the saucepan containing the raspberry mixture almost to rim in ice but do not let any water get into saucepan. Stir while mixture cools to the consistency of unbeaten egg whites; this takes about 5 minutes. Remove saucepan from water and reserve it at room temperature.

4. In a chilled bowl with chilled beaters, beat the cream until stiff. Whisk large spoonful of whipped cream into thickened raspberry mixture to lighten. Fold lightened raspberry mixture into remaining whipped cream until thoroughly blended. Spoon into non-corrosive 1-1/2 quart mold. Cover and refrigerate until set, about 3 hours.

5. Sprinkle reserved 1 cup raspberries with remaining 1/4 cup sugar; toss gently. Refrigerate, covered, until serving time.

6.   To unmold, dip the mold quickly in hot water. Now place chilled serving platter over open side of mold; invert mold, shaking slightly to loosen. Garnish with reserved chilled raspberries and their juices. Serve immediately.

Yield: *6-8 servings*

FRENCH PUDDING

1 cup dry wine
1 cup water
$\frac{1}{2}$ cup semolina
Vegetable-oil spray
$\frac{3}{4}$ cup sugar
$\frac{1}{4}$ teaspoon salt (optional)
1 egg or 2 egg whites
1 teaspoon orange flower water (optional)
4 egg whites at room temperature
Double recipe of Fresh Raspberry Sauce

1. Preheat oven 350 degree F. and spray oil on 8 cup Bundt pan or mold.
2. Combine wine and water in sauce pan using medium-high heat. Bring to a boil. Slowly add semolina, stirring constantly, until the porridge begins to thicken. Cook slowly in a covered pan using low heat, stirring constantly until very thick for about 15 minutes.
3. Remove sauce pan from heat and add sugar and salt to porridge and dissolve. By the spoonful, add porridge into beaten egg or 2 whites, blend well. Stir in orange flower water.
4. Beat 4 egg whites in a large bowl until they form stiff peaks. Stir in large spoonful of beaten whites into porridge to lighten. Pour porridge-egg white mixture over the remaining egg whites; fold together gently but thoroughly with rubber spatula.
5. Spoon mixture into prepared Bundt pan and put on the center rack of oven; pour boiling water into larger pan until it reaches level of mixture in mold. Bake until cake mixture is puffed and very lightly browned. Use wooden pick to check doneness, about 30 minutes.
6. Carefully remove pan from water bath to wire rack. Let cool. Unmold, and refrigerate, covered with plastic wrap, chill at least 2 hours.
7. Serve with generous amounts of Fresh Raspberry Sauce.

FRESH RASPBERRY SAUCE
3 cups fresh, picked clean, raspberries
$\frac{1}{3}$ cup sugar
2 tablespoons orange liqueur or fruit brandy (peach brandy works well)

You can either puree the raspberries or you can use them whole. If you have trouble with the seeds, push them through a sieve.

Dissolve the sugar and one half the raspberries in a small sauce pan. Remove and add the fresh raspberries and the liqueur or brandy. Can be served warm or cold.

RICH-RASPBERRY SOUFFLE

Here is a dessert for any time of the year.

2 tablespoons cold water
1 envelope unflavored gelatin
1-10½ ounces unfrozen raspberries or 1 ½ cups fresh raspberries
½ cup sugar
7 egg whites
1 cup heavy cream or no-fat yogurt substitute

1. Surround a 1-quart souffle dish with a long piece of waxed paper. After you fold the wax paper in half, length wise, spray with vegetable oil. Turn the oiled side inward. Tie the paper around the souffle dish and extend it 2 inches above the rim.

2. In a medium saucepan, soften gelatin in water. Add berries to gelatin with the sugar and heat, stirring, until the gelatin and sugar have dissolved. Transfer to a large bowl and chill until cool but not yet gelled.

3. Beat the whites until stiff and fold into berries. Whip the cream or yogurt and fold into berry mixture.

4. Spoon carefully into the souffle dish. The mixture should rise above the rim. Chill overnight or freeze until several hours before serving. Remove collar and serve with sauce.

FRAMBOISE SAUCE
1-10½ ounces unfrozen raspberries or 1-½ cups fresh raspberries
¼ cup sugar
2 tablespoons Framboise or Chambord (raspberry liqueur)

You can either puree the raspberries or you can use them whole. If you have trouble with the seeds, push them through a sieve.

Dissolve the sugar and one half the raspberries in a small sauce pan. Remove and add the fresh raspberries and the liqueur. Can be served warm or cold.

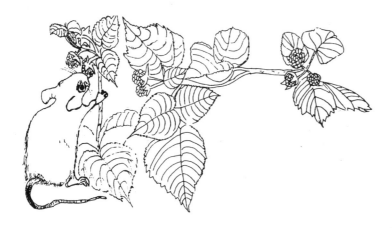

RASPBERRY & MANGO GRATIN
WITH RASPBERRY SABAYON BELVEDERE

2 peeled mangoes
²/₃ cup picked over raspberries
2 large egg yolks
2 large whole eggs
6 tablespoons sugar
3 tablespoons raspberry liqueur (Chambord or Eau-de vie de framboise)

There are two ways to cut the mango. The first way will have pictures to illustrate the cutting. Use one or the other of these techniques.

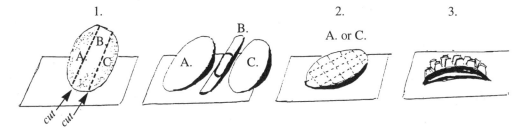

First Method:

1. Cut a thick slice, as close to the pit, off both sides.
2. On a cutting board, take the thick slice and place it skin down on the cutting board. Cut the thick slices, one at a time. Cut the long way 4 or 5 cuts into the mango flesh down to the skin, not cutting the skin. Now make cuts the opposite way 5-6 cuts down to the skin.
3. Now push the skin side up into the middle so that the square cuts in the flesh are sticking out and the mango sits inverted, with the squarish mounds facing up.
4. Place one inverted mango into a gratin dish. Top with the fresh or frozen berries.

Second Method:

Cut a thick slice off the 2 flat sides of each mango and cut each slice lengthwise into 6 slices. Using a decorative arrangement divide the slices among the buttered individual gratin dishes. Top with fresh or frozen berries.

Sabayon:

Using a medium bowl, beat the egg yolks, the whole eggs, sugar and raspberry liqueur. Set the bowl over a small saucepan of simmering water, and beat the mixture at high speed for 5 to 10 minutes, or until it is thick and foamy and very warm to the touch. Spoon the sabayon sauce generously over the fruit, covering it completely, and put the desserts under a preheated broiler about 2 inches from the heat for 30 seconds to 1 minute, or until they are browned lightly. Serve the desserts immediately.

Yield: Serves 4

RASPBERRY COBBLER

1-1/2 cups whole wheat flour
1 cup oatmeal
1/2 cup walnuts or sunflower seeds
1/8 cup poppy seeds
1/2 to 2/3 cup brown sugar
1/3 cup canola oil
1/3 cup skim milk

RASPBERRY SAUCE

1 tablespoon of lemon juice or Peach Schnapps
1/2 cup sugar
4 cups raspberries

TOPPING

2 teaspoons raw sugar
1/2 cup walnuts

1. Combine first 7 ingredients in medium bowl and pour 1/2 of mixture in a 12 x 12 inch oiled pyrex dish. Olive oil spray is best.
2. Make Raspberry Sauce and pour on top of mixture.
3. Place remainder of the mixture on top of the Raspberry Sauce, then sprinkle evenly with topping.
4. Cook in a 400 degree F. oven for approximately 15 to 20 minutes or until the top layer is brown and bubbly. Serve plain or with vanilla frozen yogurt or ice cream.

RASPBERRY APRICOT COBBLER

5 cups sliced fresh apricots (peaches or blueberries can replace apricots)
1-1/4 cups fresh or frozen raspberries
1/2 cup raw sugar
4-1/2 teaspoons cornstarch
3/4 cup oat bran
3/4 cup whole wheat flour
1/4 cup raw sugar
2 teaspoons baking powder
3/4 cup nonfat buttermilk

1. Preheat oven at 375 degrees F.
2. Make the fruit filling by mixing the fruit, sugar, and cornstarch.
3. Pour the fruit filling into a 2 quart baking dish that has been coated with a vegetable oil spray. Put aside.
4. Using a medium bowl, combine the oat bran, flour, sugar, and baking powder, and stir to mix well. Stir in the buttermilk. Drop heaping tablespoons of batter onto the fruit to make 8 biscuits.
5. Bake for 35-40 minutes, or until the fruit is bubbly and the biscuits are golden brown. If the top starts to brown too quickly cover the dish with foil for the last 10 minutes. Serve warm with vanilla nonfat frozen yogurt.

CHOCOLATE RASPBERRY MERINGUE

We save the best for last!

This is the dessert for chocolate lovers. It rivals with Meringue For Royalty as one of my favorite desserts. Great for a very special birthday. Just stick the candles in the meringue, sing "Happy Birthday" or "Long Live the King"!

MERINGUES:

4 egg whites at room temperature
pinch salt
$1/_4$ teaspoon cream of tartar
1 cup sugar
3 cups yogurt whipping cream or regular whipping cream
$1/_3$ cup confectioners sugar
6 ounces semi-sweet chocolate chips
3 tablespoons orange juice concentrate
2 10-ounce packages frozen raspberries, thawed and drained
(If you use fresh raspberries, reserve a few for garnishing)

The Meringues:

When beating the egg whites until frothy, add salt and cream of tartar. Continue beating until the whites are stiff. Using brown paper as a liner for your cookie sheet, trace 3 circles about 8 or 9 inches in diameter on the brown paper. Pour the meringues and spread evenly over the circles. Bake at 250 degrees F. for 35 to 50 minutes, or until meringues are still pliable and a pale gold color. Carefully remove from the oven and peel the brown paper from the bottom. Dry cakes on a rack. The meringues can be made a day or two ahead.

To Assemble:

Melt the chocolate bits with the orange concentrate over hot water. To assemble, place a meringue layer on serving plate and spread with a layer of melted chocolate. Spread a 3/4 inch thick layer of whipped cream and then top this with a layer of berries. A second layer of meringue goes on top, spread with chocolate, whipped cream and berries. Top it with a third layer of meringue. Frost the top and sides with whipping cream. Decorate with raspberries and melted chocolate.

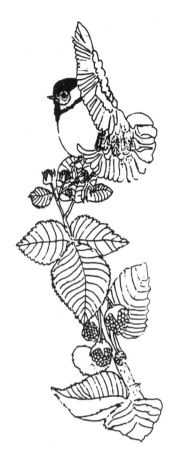

MERINGUE FOR ROYALTY

A raspberry confection and a dainty meringue, it is fit for royalty but so easy to prepare. An additional benefit is that you may make it hours ahead of dinner schedule and, if you wish to double this recipe, put it in a large mold. If you double the recipe be certain to increase the baking time in accordance with the added volume.

8 egg whites
1/2 teaspoon cream of tartar
1 cup sugar
1-1/2 cups flaked coconut
1/2 cup shaved almonds
2 teaspoons almond flavoring
1-10 ounce package defrosted, sliced raspberries
1 cup heavy cream
1 pint fresh raspberries, washed and picked over
Sugar
Sprigs mint or raspberry leaves (optional)

1. Whip egg whites and cream of tartar until foamy. Add sugar, 2 tablespoons at a time, beating after each addition. When meringue stands in stiff, glossy peaks, spoon into an ungreased, 10-cup ring mold. Do this carefully to eliminate any large air bubbles.

2. Set the mold in a shallow roasting pan filled with 1 inch of warm water. Bake 45 minutes at 250 degrees F. until meringue is set. Cool mold on a rack until the meringue settles. The meringue may remain in its mold all day at room temperature.

3. Toast coconut and shaved almonds, until golden brown in a 350 degree F. oven, stirring occasionally with a fork. Toss with almond flavoring.

4. Puree thawed berries in a blender. Beat cream until very thick but shiny. Fold into puree. Chill.

5. To serve, loosen meringue from mold with a knife that has been dipped in water to prevent tearing. Invert on serving plate and place a bowl of the raspberry cream in the center. Sprinkle the fresh berries with sugar to taste and scatter over the meringue. Sprinkle the toasted coconut/almonds over the sauce, berries, and meringue. Garnish with sprigs of mint or raspberry leaves.

Yield: Serves 8

The Story Behind the Animal Illustrations

The animals in this book do not necessarily belong in the Peaceable Kingdom as depicted in the sketches. My artistic license would tell the story with a happier ending, but the truth is the Foxy is really sweet to look at and she does have the distinction of being one the first inhabitants in my country neighborhood. She, Mrs. Foxy, had a litter of three babies this spring and she preyed upon many of the creatures who were on the raspberry scene. Our big beautiful Plymouth Rock rooster, and the white as well as the brown hen met their demise owing to satiating the appetite of Foxy. Our three Ariconda hens are still alive, as Foxy and kids moved closer to our small creek, where the living is easier. We now, of course, lock our chickens into a very secure cage nightly. Now our chicken population remains stable.

The mice are all about, in the fields, barn and patch. Whether or not mice are raspberry connoisseurs, I do not know. They probably are because raspberries are really seeds.

Bunnies frequent the lush grass around our area. Did you notice that they were not shown eating the raspberries?

The butterflies and the bees are always around the blossoms in early summer. The bees are vital, we know. The butterflies like rotting or very ripe fruit, so if they are on the raspberries, chances are that the fruit is past the point of enjoyment.

Birds frequent the patch. The new species you see is my own version of the elegant, "Raspberry Bird". I will not be surprised if you have never seen it.

The blue jays and robins do love raspberries as much as I do. Chickadees and quail, NO. But because I LOVE to draw birds they are there, and you can imagine that they love raspberries as much as you and I!

Chipmunks and bears love the wild berries too and in my next edition, if there is one, they will be part of the illustrations. Turn the page to see our patch!

And
Our Patch Too!

INDEX

A note from . . . .

_____

_____

_____

_____

_____

_____

_____

_____

_____

A notecard from The Complete Colorado Raspberry Story - with over 140 delicious recipes.

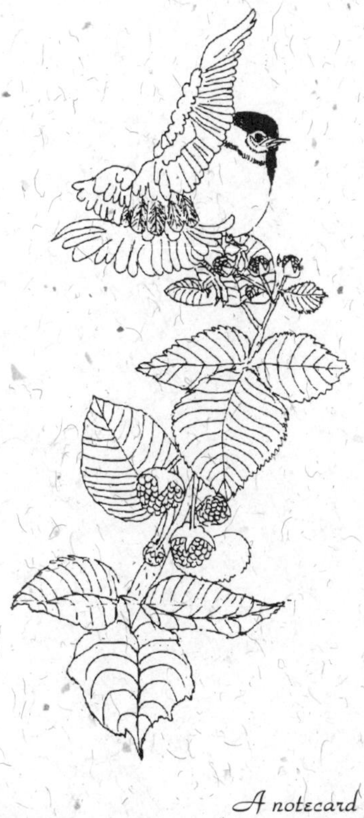

A note from . . . .

_____

_____

_____

_____

_____

_____

_____

_____

_____

_____

_____

A notecard from The Complete Colorado Raspberry Story with over 140 delicious recipes.

A note from . . . .

_____

_____

_____

_____

_____

_____

_____

_____

_____

A notecard from The Complete Colorado Raspberry Story - with over 140 delicious recipes.

A note from . . . .

_____

_____

_____

_____

_____

_____

_____

_____

_____

_____

A notecard from The Complete Colorado Raspberry Story with over 140 delicious recipes.

A note from . . . .

_____
_____
_____
_____
_____

_____
_____
_____
_____

A notecard from The Complete Colorado Raspberry Story - with over 140 delicious recipes.

A note from . . . .

_____
_____
_____
_____
_____
_____
_____

A notecard from The Complete Colorado Raspberry Story with over 140 delicious recipes.